Get Writing!!

The Total Writing Program

Book 2 Grades 4-5
Main Ideas in Paragraphs

This book is dedicated to the teachers who worked with us over the years, refining our profession's understanding of how to teach children and adolescents to write well. We particularly appreciate Suzanne Jackson, Ellen Phaneuf, and Diane Rocha.

Editor: Shirley J. Durst
Cover/Page Layout: Kirstin Simpson
Book Design: Educational Media Services

ISBN 1-57022-197-9

Printed in the United States of America.

Leif Fearn's work with children and writing had its genesis many years ago when his sixth-grade students' fiction ended up as a full page of stories in the local newspaper. Later, in both the Southwest and Northwest, he had the opportunity to emphasize literacy development as a trainer of Head Start teachers and aides. His early applications of creative thinking to existing curriculum, however, eventually led to his and Nancy's conception of Balanced Writing instruction.

Nancy Farnan's teaching began with middle and secondary students in the Midwest. Early in her career, she experienced her students' learning to write as watching buds opening to full bloom—the changes were observable, tangible, and powerful. She was impressed by the power her students discovered as they became increasingly effective writers.

A little over a decade ago, Leif and Nancy began to use their experiences, along with those of several outstanding teachers and colleagues, to develop the concept of Balanced Writing instruction. For a decade they have worked with teachers in the Writing Institute for Teachers at San Diego State University, refining and adding to their conception of what a Balanced Writing program would look and sound like. They have authored and co-authored many books and articles on writing and regularly lead workshops to promote Balanced Writing instruction and literacy.

Today, Leif and Nancy teach at San Diego State University, where they share an office in the School of Teacher Education. As key figures in the development of Balanced Writing instruction, they have devoted their professional lives to literacy and the development of writing skills. Married, Leif and Nancy live in San Diego, California, where they meet regularly with the professional writers' community.

Contents

About This Book

 The Get Writing!! Series

The **Get Writing!!** series is a comprehensive, teacher-friendly, Balanced Writing program for kindergarten through fifth grade.

Balanced Writing instruction was born in the late 1970s as Developmental Writing, an application of creative thinking skills to teaching and learning basic school skills and content (Fearn, 1976). Balanced Writing instruction focuses specific attention on balancing three components of writing associated with learning to write well:

1. The **CONTENT** of writing:
   - Sentence thinking and writing
   - Thinking and writing in relationships between and among sentences
   - Thinking and writing in paragraphs
   - Progressive mastery of writing for various purposes across the genres
   - Progressive mastery of writing conventions
   - Assessment and editing
2. The **PROCESSES** involved in learning and writing:
   - Written interactions between planning and drafting and between drafting and revision
   - Control of the cognitive devices of attention
   - Conceptualization
   - Application of specific creative thinking skills
3. The **TIME** demands associated with learning to write well:
   Practice in Balanced Writing instruction should be 10 percent of the instructional week, or up to 100 to 150 clock minutes of instructional time per week.

 What's Inside This Book?

The lessons in the **Get Writing!!** series relate directly to every student in the room. They specify student writing behaviors, include multiple procedures for the assessment of writing, and describe, in the most explicit terms, what teachers and students can do to achieve each objective.

Get Writing!! Book 2 Grades 4-5, Main Ideas in Paragraphs, focuses on bringing students to mature writing by teaching them to use paragraphs as a tool for organizing main ideas. Students first learn to write and recognize main ideas in multiple sentences and then to organize these main ideas into paragraphs. They then learn to write subsequent paragraphs to enhance the main ideas, and to use these skills in report writing, opinion and persuasive writing, story writing, drafting and revision, informal and formal letter writing, and autobiographical writing.

Get Writing!!
Main Ideas in Paragraphs

Lesson Design

Each lesson in this book begins with Information for the Teacher and with a section of detailed instructions and examples for conducting the lesson. These examples include a synopsis of student/teacher dialogue based on actual sessions with children and adolescents. For identification purposes, the teacher's comments and questions are enclosed in quotations, and the students' comments are enclosed in parentheses.

Each lesson also includes the following:

- Daily Writing Activities
- Applications of the Lesson Across the Curriculum
- Applications for English Language Learners
- Reproducible Language Activity Sheets for classroom use

As with all other skills, writing skills can be acquired at more than one level of sophistication. Thinking in sentences, for instance, is introduced in ***Get Writing!! Kindergarten***, then applied to writing in ***Get Writing!! Books 1 and 2 Grades 2-3***, and again in ***Get Writing!! Books 1 and 2 Grades 4-5***. Certain activities are appropriate at any grade level. If students claim they "did this last year," they can be reminded that what they remember about writing from last year will give them a running start this year.

Hints for Supporting a Balanced Writing Program

- **Writing instruction should focus young writers' attention on creation (the thinking in writing) and on making the scribal part of writing as automatic as possible.** In writing, practice makes automatic, so some instructional processes should emphasize speed and quantity.
- **Practice makes permanent.** Every instance of writing, no matter the context, the reason, the audience, the genre, the authenticity—every one—is an instance of practice. If we want good writing from our first-, fifth-, and tenth-graders, we have to ensure that they write well every time. Our piano teachers and football coaches have the right idea, but mere practice doesn't make perfect; perfect practice makes perfect.
- **In writing instruction, as in all instruction, certain basic principles of teaching and learning must not be compromised.** First, learners must understand what is being taught. They must understand what they are supposed to do, and how they are supposed to do it. Secondly, good instruction takes advantage of, and honors, the prior knowledge that learners bring to school. Third, because children have three options in the classroom (to approach, to avoid, or to ignore), good teachers make sure most of the children achieve nearly all of the time. This virtually precludes avoiding and ignoring.

Get Writing!!
Main Ideas in Paragraphs

- **Call activities by their right names and frame directions in the vocabulary of writing.**

  Example: "That's a sentence, Eric. Read it again. Everyone, listen to Eric's sentence."

- **Avoid complex definitions.** For example, if you want a complex sentence, it isn't necessary to define dependent and independent clauses and the relationship(s) between the two. Instead, prompt students to think of a sentence in which the first word is ***although***. Then, direct them to listen to examples from other students in the room. Call attention to accurate models and reinforce.

- **Never give more time to write than young writers need.** If they are given five minutes, four will need six; if they are given six, three of the four will need seven. If they are given one minute, they'll think they can't do it, but most will. Everyone, novice and expert alike, can produce written language a whole lot faster, and better, in fact, than they think they can. An important part of learning to write is experiencing our own ability to achieve.

- **All writers must take full responsibility for spelling accurately, but don't let students' inability to spell a word correctly interfere with writing their draft.** At this point, the message to students must be, "Spell as well as you can."

- **Everything in this book is about fluency, precision, quantity, and quality, at the same time.** Getting it down on paper and getting it right are not opposites, and neither one compromises the other. Monitor students' writing by standing behind them as they read aloud.

  Example: "Put a comma right here, Cheryl. Boys and girls, remember that we always use commas when we write sentences that contain items in a series."

- **Avoid putting young writers in the position of having to live up to perfection.** Rather than saying, "That's the best paragraph in the world, Ramon," say, "That's a terrific paragraph, Ramon. Read it again."

- **Make sure that most of the writing is both oral and written (scribal).** Part of learning to write is establishing the sound of good writing.

  Example: "Read it again, Margo, and everyone listen to the sound of Margo's sentence."

Portfolios

A portfolio is a collection of work, often one's "Best Efforts." There is little or no reason for having writing portfolios in classrooms where children and young adolescents don't write much, but in classrooms where they do, they need a place to keep and organize their work.

Young writers write an enormous amount in this program. They write every day across content areas and through the genres, both collaboratively and alone. Youngsters who write this much need a place to collect, organize, and reflect upon their work. It is recommended that each student in this program keep and maintain a writing portfolio. (Farnan and Fearn, 1994).

Applications for English Language Learners

Every lesson in the **Get Writing!!** series has a section describing applications for children who do not speak English as a native language. Our experience and research shows that with non-native speakers of English the Balanced Writing instruction represented in this program is successful. The oral language component of the program is embedded in every lesson and is especially important for students whose native language is not English.

Application to Children and Young Adolescents with Special Needs

The first formal study of the impact of Balanced Writing instruction was conducted with learning disabled elementary school children (Prior, 1979). Focusing on developmental student performance tends to cut through the various "disabling" conditions. Given prior assessment of suitability to the skill level of the students, the activities in the **Get Writing!!** series are entirely appropriate for special needs youngsters.

Home Schoolers

Balanced Writing instruction has been used successfully by home school parents for many years. It is linguistically rigorous and intellectually demanding. It can be handled on a whole class, small group, or individual basis. The procedures associated with each lesson in this book are clear and focus on the developmental performance of young writers. While no collection of instructional materials is appropriate for everyone under all circumstances, this program contains literacy activities that have been used under a vast array of circumstances, including the home school.

Writing Main Ideas in Multiple Sentences

—Eventually young writers need to understand that the primary purpose of the paragraph is organization.

Information for the Teacher

For young writers, part of the complexity of the concept of main idea is the fact that most often main idea is in the process of becoming; it is emerging or being formed, even as the writing is being invented and constructed.

Though many young writers believe that main idea exists before the writing, main ideas often develop as the writing unfolds, growing from small ones in single sentences to larger ones in multiple sentences.

It is true that writers can, and often do, write paragraphs that contain main ideas they have planned before they begin to write. More often, however, main ideas become apparent to writers during the writing. Good writers find these main ideas and organize them into properly sequenced paragraphs.

Writing Main Ideas in Multiple Sentences helps young writers understand how they can gain control over the paragraph. It does not teach procedures for writing paragraphs. It is absolutely not a format or procedure for how to write paragraphs. It highlights the control and management of main ideas, allowing students to experience the development of main idea as the paragraph develops.

Objective

Young writers will arrange ideas into multiple sentences and discuss the main idea(s) that emerge. They will also arrange ideas into multiple sentences in which the main idea is given.

Writing Main Ideas in Multiple Sentences

Conducting the Lesson

1. **Direct students to mentally construct three given ideas into two related sentences.**

   Example: "Remember when we wrote single sentences based on ideas on the board? We're going to do something like that again, but this time we're writing multiple sentences about an idea. I want you to think of a way to arrange the ideas on the board [**old man, weather, vehicle**] into two related sentences. Don't write anything on paper. Just write in your head."

2. **Ask volunteers to share their mental constructions aloud.**

   Example: (The old man's car stopped in a rain storm. His car wouldn't start again because the motor was wet.)

3. **Using a student's sentences as the example, briefly review the idea of related sentences in paragraphs.**

   Example: "You thought of two related sentences using the three ideas. Now, share just your second sentence." (**His car wouldn't start again because the motor was wet.**) "You don't tell us in that sentence who 'he' is, do you?" (I don't have to because the first sentence says that he's an old man.) "That is the best definition of related sentences. The two sentences are held together, or related, with the first word of his second sentence. Who can remember what the word is?" (***His***.) "Yes, the pronoun, ***His***, connects with ***old man*** in the first sentence to the second sentence, so we know they are the same person in both sentences. The two sentences are related."

4. **Ask the student to identify the main idea of his/her two related sentences.** Listen to several other examples to make sure the idea of related sentences is clear to everyone.

   Example: "What is your double sentence string about? What's its main idea?" (A man got stuck in the storm and can't get out?) "Yes, your two sentences have a main idea."

5. **Direct students to mentally construct a third related sentence to go with their two previous sentences.**

   Example: "Now let's take it to the next stage. Remember your two sentences. I want you to add a third sentence. Write a third sentence in your head so you will have three related sentences. I'll give you several seconds."

Arrange the ideas **milk**, **pasture**, and **stroll** in two related sentences. What is the main idea in the double sentence string? Write the third sentence in the series to continue the main idea. Write a sentence that can complete the paragraph.

Writing Main Ideas in Multiple Sentences

People who write well have more than minimal control of their own mental processes. They often frame whole ideas mentally and play with various ways the idea might be written.

Memory is a very sophisticated and critical mental process. Remembering the three related sentences will be difficult for students at first. However, with practice in context, as described in this activity, they will progressively gain greater control.

6. **Listen to several triple sentence strings, noting main idea along the way.** Then give students two minutes to write their sentences on paper.

   Example: "What is your main idea?" (It's that the man didn't want to go to the store anyway, so he's not mad about the rain.) "Now write your three related sentences on paper. I'll give you two minutes."

7. **Let students know when there is a half-minute left.** After that half-minute, allow another 15-20 seconds for completion, then ask for volunteers to read their sentences.

8. **Listen to several children while reading over their shoulders.** Read silently with them and notice mechanical attributes of their writing.

In the middle elementary grades, it is time for students to use the basic conventions of capitalization and punctuation properly.

Part of learning to write is becoming automatic with basic mechanical conventions and spelling high-frequency words correctly. Young writers must be held responsible so they can learn to hold themselves responsible.

9. **Take 15-20 minutes to conduct more triple-sentence sessions, calling explicit attention to main idea.** One variation is to have a child read a three-sentence piece and identify the main idea. (**The old man got stuck in the rain. His car slipped off the road near the creek. He was really scared because he didn't want to fall into the creek.**)

   Example: "Read your three sentences." [Student reads.] "What's the main idea of your first sentence?" (It's that he couldn't get his car out of the ditch.) "Now what's the main idea of the first and second sentences together?" (It's about where he got stuck.) "And what's the main idea of all three sentences together?" (He was scared he might fall into the creek and get washed away.)

Writing Main Ideas in Multiple Sentences

10. **Ask others in the room if they agree about the main idea, then review the process of revising sentences to meet an intended main idea.**

    Example: "If you want the main idea to be the man's fright at being washed down the swollen creek in his car, and your sentences didn't say that to the rest of us, what would you do?" (I would have to rewrite something to make sure.) "Right. You know what your main idea is supposed to be. If that isn't the main idea for your readers, you have some revisions to make. How would you raise what you wrote to make sure your readers know about the man's fear?"

In the classroom, students usually write for themselves and their teacher, but they will eventually have to write for an audience, and often their peers. Responses from the audience demonstrate whether the writing works.

11. **In subsequent sessions, solicit statements about the main idea plus elaborations in the form of a sentence to add to their triple sentence string to make it a complete paragraph.** In later sessions, ask students to write a fourth and fifth sentence that maintain the original main idea of the triple.

Remember, paragraphs are as long as the writer's main idea. A "big" main idea may need more sentences.

12. **Eventually, when the final sentence has been written and the paragraph seems complete, ask students to think what might be the main idea of the next paragraph.** Variations on this activity include: What might be the first sentence of the next paragraph? What might be the main idea of the paragraph that came just before the one you just wrote? What might be the last sentence in the paragraph just before the one you just wrote?

Conduct this activity on a regular basis until everyone, or nearly everyone easily, if not automatically, can write a three-sentence piece and then add another sentence that "fills out" the main idea. Students should also then be able to add the main idea of the next paragraph.

This isn't the only paragraph thinking and writing opportunity students will get in the fourth and fifth grades. Remember that they will also be writing stories, reports, and other communications, even as they are working explicitly on their paragraphs.

Writing Main Ideas in Multiple Sentences

 Daily Writing Activities

Any combination of prompts or idea words can promote multiple sentence writing for this activity. Below are several combinations that have been used in middle and upper elementary grades. You might also use words from the spelling program and vocabulary word lists from content areas as idea words.

1. shirt
button
float
2. mud
seat
window
3. sign
corner
container
4. basket
folder
baggage
5. cover
paint
abbey
6. hawk
cave
gate
7. nail
statue
building
8. glass
cord
phone
9. magnet
clasp
critter
10. woman
vent
bastion
11. running
cute
kite
12. pipe
water
street
13. aid
plastic
book
14. sheet
frame
tractor
15. gentleman
board
cruel
16. bird
dirt
log
17. rusty
yellow
reading
18. paper
cup
pencil
19. pink
meander
pillow
20. girl
doorway
fashion

Writing Main Ideas in Multiple Sentences

Across the Curriculum

This lesson can easily be applied throughout the curriculum. To compliment a music unit, for example, the direction to students might be, "Think of three related sentences in which you arrange the musical terms *chord, clef, staff.*"

Consider other combinations of three ideas for three related sentences.

civil	circulation	cirrus	plane
revolution	blood	cumulous	solid
conflict	systems	billowing	figure

English Language Learners

There is a difference between the language children often use to talk with one another and the language teachers and texts use to communicate at school. The **B**asic **I**nterpersonal **C**ommunication **S**kill (**BICS**) level of language, which children acquire to communicate and get along, is a very useful application of language in context. On the playground, where everyone needs to understand how to play the game, there is vocabulary, syntax, and lots of body language. There, the language used to get the point across isn't as important as the point, itself. There is little or no anxiety, or affective filter, and the motive is explicitly authentic to the speakers' needs.

In the classroom this changes. There, the language load is **C**ognitive, the purpose is **A**cademic, the **L**anguage demands are more formal, and the objective is **P**roficiency (**CALP**). There is no body language. The motive is seldom very authentic to learners' felt or perceived needs. No matter how carefully the teacher plans, and no matter how warmly (s)he behaves in the classroom, there is a kind of anxiety not found on the playground and in the neighborhood.

These differences between informal and formal language must be accommodated. Accommodation does not mean using basic interpersonal language to communicate school content. These are different language environments, and it's important to help young people negotiate both effectively.

In **Writing Main Ideas in Multiple Sentences** there is talk and listening with attention to the sounds of language. English writing instruction in a classroom where half or more of the children speak a native language other than English is never easy, but it can be effective if it is student-selected, if the affective filter is lowered, and if the language is authentic (first auditory, then scribal).

This interactive activity focuses deliberate attention on the formal language of school in a non-threatening manner. This form of language (related sentences) can be mastered quickly in English because it occurs in other languages, as well. The context is school content and the terminology that expresses it is in both oral and written language.

Language Activity Sheet

Writing Main Ideas in Multiple Sentences

1. Write a sentence that contains the idea of ***temperature***, but do not use that word.

____

____

In a short phrase, write the main idea of your sentence.

____

2. Write two related sentences that contain the ideas ***temperature*** and ***play***. Do not use these words.

____

____

In a short phrase, write the main idea of your two related sentences.

____

3. Write three related sentences that contain a character, but do not use that word, plus the ideas of ***play*** and ***temperature***.

____

____

In a short phrase, write the main idea of your three related sentences.

____

4. If the three related sentences do not complete the main idea, write a fourth sentence that will complete the main idea.

____

____

5. Write what you think might be the main idea of the paragraph that comes right after the one you wrote above.

____

____

6. Now that you have thought what might be the main idea of the next paragraph, write what you think could be the first sentence of that paragraph.

____

____

2 Paragraph Completion: Writing to Main Ideas

—Paragraphs written by good writers are rarely collections of the component parts of paragraphs defined in language arts books.

 Information for the Teacher

Sentences and paragraphs are both arrangements of particular elements. Students in elementary school know they can write sentences without knowing the names, roles, and positions of these elements, but are often led to believe that they cannot write paragraphs without knowing them.

Elementary students learn, for instance, that sentences have subjects and predicates, adjectives, objects of prepositions, and independent clauses. Most students write sentences that work pretty well most of the time, in spite of the fact that they don't remember the names of the component parts. That is because no one, not even English teachers, use a grammatical template to write sentences.

While both sentences and paragraphs have identical purposes and very similar design characteristics, young writers rarely have an opportunity to take advantage of what they know about sentences to learn about paragraphs. Most students begin paragraph writing before they can think in and talk in paragraphs.

Rarely does a teacher refer to the main idea in sentences or in more than one paragraph. Main idea in sentences is usually called the "subject," and it isn't usually defined as what the sentence is about. When students begin to write paragraphs, the terminology often changes from "subject" to "main idea." Furthermore, there is often little or no explanation of the organizational role of the paragraph in writing. We must provide a bridge of understanding from what students know about sentences to what they will be doing with paragraphs. **Paragraph Completion: Writing to Main Ideas** explicitly addresses these problems.

 Objective

Young writers, whether in the early fourth or late fifth grade, will use a paragraph format to think about main idea, and complete the paragraph to show that main idea. They will, as well, speculate on the main idea of the following, or previous, paragraph, and they will write at least one sentence that reflects that second paragraph.

Paragraph Completion: Writing to Main Ideas

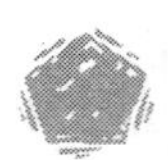

Conducting the Lesson

1. **Direct students' attention to sentence stems on the board or overhead.**

   Example: "Look at what I have prepared for you on the chalkboard:"
   The sky was blue and the temperature cool as we began our climb. The first part of the slope wasn't very steep, so we ... Then the trail turned straight up, and ... It wasn't long before we had to ... That's when we saw ...

2. **Ask students to volunteer what they think the main idea of the paragraph might be.** Pause for thinking time.

   Example: "What might be the main idea of this paragraph?" (Climbing mountains. I think it's about some people climbing a mountain. Maybe it's about a storm coming, and they'll be caught up there.) "That would be what happens next. What's happening in the paragraph on the board?" (It's about some people climbing a mountain, and it gets hard to climb as they get higher.) "Everyone, think of the main idea of the paragraph. Think what it might be about. This paragraph has how many sentences?" (Five.) "Right, and the first one is already written, so write that one as your first sentence. The rest of them are only started, and you must finish them so your main idea becomes clear. Remember, your main idea must be clear to your readers, so be careful about how you write the sentences. You have three minutes."

3. **When half the students are finished writing, announce that 30 seconds remain to finish their paragraphs.** When the time is up, ask for volunteers to read their paragraphs and to identify the main idea.

Presented with a lead sentence plus at least three sentence stems, young writers consider what the main idea would be and complete the paragraph. Once they complete the paragraph, they then speculate on the main idea of the next paragraph and write portions of that one, as well.

Paragraph Completion: Writing to Main Ideas

Example: "Who will read their paragraph?" (**The sky was deep blue and the weather was nice as we began to climb the mountain. The first part wasn't very steep. So we didn't have to rest because we didn't get out of breath. Then the trail turned straight up, and we had to hold onto each other to keep from falling. It wasn't long before we had to be resting all the time because we were tired and sweating and out of breath. That's when we looked up and saw we didn't even have half of the mountain done yet.**)

"What is the main idea of your paragraph?" (It's about the people climbing the mountain and it gets harder and harder.) "Will they get to the top?" (Yes.) "Would you like to get them to the top in one more paragraph?" (Sure.) "Go on, then. Write your next paragraph. We'll listen to several more while you're writing."

4. **With each reading, direct students to write the next paragraph.** After several readings to establish the pattern, instruct everyone to think what might happen in the next paragraph.

   Example: "See if the first sentence tells what the main idea might be. Write the second sentence in the paragraph, and the third and so forth, until you think the paragraph is finished. I will be asking what your main idea is, so you want to think about that, too."

If this direction seems too complex, step back one level and emphasize only the paragraph completion format. Direct them eventually to begin thinking about the next paragraph by speculating about the main idea and/or the first sentence.

5. **On another day, pose a new paragraph writing stem.** Ask students to think of the main idea of the paragraph, and then write the main idea in their heads. Pause for the thinking, then ask them to write the main idea in not more than six words.

   Example: I spend a lot of time in my bedroom. It has blue … There are shelves near … I like to listen to … My room is …

6. **Once most students are writing, begin writing a paragraph using the same stem.** This gives the few who are not off the ground something to read and maybe an idea or two for writing.

Even if students merely copy what you write on the board, they can speculate on the following paragraph or its main idea. This activity is about bridging the gap from sentence thinking to paragraph thinking. If the gap is bridged often enough, young writers are more likely to attempt the leap.

7. **Conduct readings and conversations about the main ideas in their paragraph.** Also discuss subsequent main ideas and the first sentence of the next paragraph.
8. **Suggest that young writers revise their paragraph(s) to make a Best Effort worthy of posting on the Best Effort Board.**

Have a stamp made that reads Best Effort. Stamp student papers for posting and display them for a day.

9. **Conduct this activity on regular occasions throughout the year.** As the year progresses, these activities should become two- and three-paragraph pieces.

Paragraph Completion: Writing to Main Ideas

 Daily Writing Activities

1. A cow is a farm animal. It can be brown … Most of the time we know about cows because … The milk is …
2. Flying on an airplane can be very exciting. At an airport …The planes … Mostly, people use airplanes because …
3. The streets in a big city can be very exciting. There are people … Some of the people live … The stores and shops … And on some streets there are lots of …
4. Everyone in the room heard the noise at the same time. They all ran … Outside they saw … No one wanted to go out right away because … They returned to their seats and …
5. My favorite kind of reading is stories. I like stories best when … The best story I ever read is … The main character is best known for …
6. Riding a bicycle on a cool day is the best thing to do. The wind feels … I can hear … I can feel … It makes me think of …
7. I remember when I tried to learn how to … It was frustrating when … But I remember working … Then one day … I felt …

Paragraph Completion: Writing to Main Ideas

 Across the Curriculum

This lesson can easily be applied to writing in any content area. For example, having read about, experimented with, and discussed a scientific concept, students might then write what the experiment revealed or what the concept means:

> **A lever is a simple machine. There is the rod, or lever, which is ... To lift one corner of a big box, one end of the level ... Then the fulcrum should be placed ... If you push down on the end of the lever, ...**

The same procedure can applied to a history unit on the American Revolution:

> **In the American Revolution, the colonists revolted against England. They wanted to ... George Washington was ... He stayed with the soldiers during ... After the war, George Washington ...**

In each instance, encourage students to write a two- or three-paragraph piece to practice cohesion from paragraph to paragraph and to explore as much content as they can.

 English Language Learners

Using the following example, and the procedures above, young writers can use personal experiences as paragraph writing cues by arranging words and phrases. (Ramirez, A.G. (1995). *Creating Contexts for Second Language Acquisition: Theory and Methods*. White Plains, NY: Longmont, pp. 282-283.)

In the morning	**I study**	**watch TV**
Then	**work**	**listen to the radio**
At noon	**play**	**visit friends**
Later	**shop**	**do homework**

Paragraph Completion: Writing to Main Ideas promotes thinking about the transitions that occur from paragraph to paragraph. Every time students think about the concept of main idea and complete the sentences in this activity, they regularly practice writing paragraphs and experience the linking of ideas across paragraphs.

English language learners can depend on **Paragraph Completion** to give them a paragraph every time. As they write more and more, and elaborate in subsequent paragraphs, they will need the artificial format less and less.

Language Activity Sheet

Paragraph Completion: Writing to Main Ideas

1. Read the writing in the box, and think about what the main idea might be. Write what you think might be the main idea in the space below the box.

> **As I walked down the street, I saw a puppy. It was running toward ... I glanced around, but ... When I saw what was going to happen, I ... I'm glad I saw the puppy because ...**

____

2. In the spaces below, write the whole five-sentence paragraph. Your paragraph doesn't have to be about the main idea you wrote in the space above, but it may.

____

____

____

____

____

3. Read your paragraph to a partner and ask what (s)he thinks is the main idea. Write in the space below what (s)he said is the main idea.

____

4. What do you think might be the main idea of the paragraph that comes next. Think about that for a few seconds, and write the main idea in the space below.

____

5. Write what you think might be the first sentence of that next paragraph.

____

____

6. In the spaces below, write the rest of the paragraph.

____

____

____

____

____

3 Finding Paragraphs: Arranging Sentences

—To write cohesive paragraphs, writers must construct mental connections between and among sentences.

Information for the Teacher

Finding Paragraphs: Arranging Sentences causes students to use paragraphs as organizational devices. As writers routinely attest, they invaribly find paragraphs in what they are writing, rather than write paragraphs for which they have prepared main ideas. This is why most good paragraphs in literature don't contain all of the elements of paragraphs found in fourth- and eighth-grade textbooks.

A paragraph always has a main idea, however. And, often there is a topic sentence, especially when the writing is in certain content areas. But just as often there is no topic sentence. Most characteristically, it is absent in fiction. It's even sometimes absent from the opinion page of the daily newspaper.

It isn't wrong to teach about topic sentences, various kinds of medial and terminal sentences, and transitions. But young writers must understand that all writing is context-specific. Whether or not a paragraph is arranged in five sentences with a topic sentence and a summary sentence depends mostly on the topic and the purpose of writing.

This activity broadens the range of ways in which young writers can understand how to think in and write in paragraphs. It makes both reading and writing demands on young writers. The reading demands promote language behaviors critical in paragraph writing. When arranging sentences in sequence, the writer must read all the sentences and comprehend each in a literal manner.

However, literal comprehension does not tell the reader why one sentence comes after another. What the reader decides about the relationship between the two sentences is based on inferential comprehension, or the connection the reader constructs.

To write cohesive paragraphs, writers must construct mental connections between and among sentences. In this activity, they must pay attention to connections in related sentences and construct the connections for sentences already written. In the previous activity, young writers engaged in behaviors associated with writing paragraphs. Here they engage in behaviors associated with finding paragraphs. Between the writing and the finding, a broad range of paragraph thinking and writing actions is learned and used.

Objective

Young writers, faced with unordered sentences, will arrange them in sequence, and then determine the main idea(s) in the sequence. Finally, they will rewrite the paragraph(s) on their own terms.

Finding Paragraphs: Arranging Sentences

Conducting the Lesson

1. **Compile sets of 8 to 12 single sentences onto 3" X 5" cards.**

Select a two- or three-paragraph piece from a content area book, call it Set I, and write each sentence on a separate card. Write "Set I," for instance, on each card in set one, then "Set II" on the next set, and so forth to make sure the sentences don't get mixed up.

Example:

Set I

Many Navajo people live on a reservation that includes part of Arizona, New Mexico, and Utah.

The Navajo Reservation is as large as the state of West Virginia.

Navajo people work with silver to make jewelry and wool from their sheep to weave rugs.

Their tribal capital is called Window Rock.

Other Navajo people live in cities and towns all across the United States.

Over one hundred thousand Navajo people live on the reservation.

Navajo people are also lawyers, doctors, teachers, politicians, and business leaders.

In Window Rock, the tribe conducts its business affairs and tribal government.

2. **Place an envelope of sentences on every desk in the room.** Instruct students to leave the envelope on their desks until they receive a signal.

Arrange the sentence cards in sequence, and break the sequence into main ideas. Then, write the paragraph(s) in a way that you think creates the best meaning.

Finding Paragraphs: Arranging Sentences

On an overhead projector, lay out eight sentences, move them around, establish a sequence, and separate the sentences into main ideas. Then distribute the envelopes. Or, first use the overhead to show reading and sequencing, direct students to establish a sequence, and then model finding the main idea before they work with their material.

Example: "Open your envelope and take out the cards. Your first task is to read the sentences and put them in order. Find the sentence you think should be the first one, then the second, the third, and so forth until you have them in order."

3. **As soon as almost everyone has a sequence, direct students to notice if their sentences contain more than one main idea.** Make sure they understand that they may use all of the sentences as written, they may leave out one or two, or they may write one or two new ones.

   Example: "You have all read your sentences over and over, so you know exactly what the piece is about. I'm interested in whether you see more than one main idea in your sequence. Read it over and see if there is more than one. If you find more than one main idea, break the sequence into main ideas."

4. **Finally, rewrite the paragraphs on the overhead or on the board in words more like your own, and direct students to do the same.** The end result for nearly everyone is a multiple paragraph piece that reflects their own thinking and rewriting.

5. **Conduct the entire activity in one sitting.** The first time may consume up to 15-20 minutes as the children learn the process. Each subsequent session can be conducted essentially as the one explained above, or you can distribute the envelopes and give 15 minutes to complete the entire task.

Finding Paragraphs: Arranging Sentences

Daily Writing Activities

Card sets focusing on content area texts or other valued concepts can be made by both teachers and students. Making and using the card sets connect students with content in deliberate ways. An example of a social studies card set is shown earlier in the procedures on p. 27. A different source of sentences can come from an article in a magazine.

Example:

It is winter, and high school students are beginning to think about making their applications to college.

Students all over the United States are working on their applications.

They are talking to their high school advisors for information about colleges and how to apply.

The deadline for applying to most colleges is January.

In December, they have to work especially hard.

They have to think of things to put into their applications to make themselves look as good as possible.

They have to write excellent essays about who they are and what they want to study.

It is often very stressful for they are only seventeen years old.

Direct students to read every sentence several times and construct ways to make them relate to each other. In the process, have them construct the meaning of the paragraph(s). Because of the deliberate reading and meaning construction, they learn something about the material. However, the real purpose of the activity is finding and revising paragraphs.

Finding Paragraphs: Arranging Sentences

 Across the Curriculum

Finding Paragraphs: Arranging Sentences has clear applications for writing across the curriculum. The writing in content areas can be used for sequencing sentences, finding main ideas, and rewriting.

Example: Direct students to consider the six- to eight-sentence pieces students write as directions for accomplishing a specific task. One fifth-grader wrote the following directions for drawing a rectangle:

> "First, make a line from east to west. Make another line from east to west right under the first line. Make the two lines from east to west the same length. Then make a straight line that connects one end of the two east to west lines. Then make another straight line that connects the other end of the two east to west lines."

If these sentences were presented out of order, young writers would attempt to construct several different meanings. First, they can't make a sequence until they figure out what this piece is about. Then they have to create an order by constructing the sense of the piece. Of course, by finding the sense, making the arrangement, and revising, they will also construct a very explicit direction for drawing rectangles.

Finding Paragraphs: Arranging Sentences is especially useful when we want youngsters to read a complex passage very carefully. Readers will recognize these sentences from Jack London's opening paragraph of *The Call of the Wild* (Pocket Books, 1982).

Example:

Buck did not read the newspapers.	They would have told him that trouble was brewing.
Strong dogs with heavy muscles and long, warm hair were in trouble.	All of the dogs from San Diego north to Puget Sound were in trouble.
Men found gold in the north where the heavy snow and cold were.	Dogs were the transportation system there.
Dogs pulled the sleds that carried the men and their supplies.	Hundreds of men were looking for dogs.
Buck would have known all that if he could read the newspaper.	But dogs couldn't read, and Buck was one of those big strong dogs with a heavy coat.

This activity, applied to literature, promotes careful reading.

 English Language Learners

One clear benefit of a sentence arrangement activity is the allowance for deliberate reading and thinking. There is no premium on speed, and young writers are in a position to think about relationships between and among sentence ideas.

One of the major objectives of teaching writing is to promote attention to audience. To help accomplish this, student work may be posted for everyone to read or may be published in classroom books.

Each story can be also used as content for sentence arrangement. Distribute six to eight 3" X 5" cards to everyone in the room. Direct students to find a place in a story (or essay, report, and so forth) where they have written a six- to eight-sentence passage that makes sense all by itself. Tell students to work on that piece until it is as good as it can be. Explain that readers will have to figure out the meaning on the basis of the quality of the writing.

When they have their passage written as clearly as they possibly can, direct them to write one sentence per 3" X 5" card. Instruct them to code each card according to the owner, so they can be identified.

Cardpacks can then be distributed around the room. Give everyone multiple opportunities to read, think, sequence, and rewrite language that comes from the experiences and ideas that represent the diversity in the classroom.

Language Activity Sheet

Finding Paragraphs: Arranging Sentences

Write each of the sentences in the box on a separate 3" X 5" card. Be sure to copy each sentence exactly as it is written in the box.

The middle part of the United States is called the heartland.	It is the land of farmers who grow the wheat.
The wheat is what people use to make bread and cereal.	In the heartland there are small towns and large cities.
Cows graze in the pastures as the farmers plant in the fall and harvest in the summer.	The farmers live in houses often surrounded by barns and silos.
The roads through the heartland have travelers in their cars and farmers with their trucks and machinery.	The heartland is a place of hard work.

1. Arrange your set of sentence cards on the desk in front of you. Read the cards and try to figure what they might be about. As you read, select what you think is the best first sentence in the set. Then select what you think is the best second sentence in the set, then the third, the fourth, and so forth until you have the sentence cards arranged in order from the first to the last.

2. When you have the sentence cards arranged in order from the first to the last, read through all of the cards and decide if there is more than one main idea. If the way you have the cards arranged is all one main idea, you have one paragraph. If there is more than one main idea, you will have more than one paragraph.

3. In the spaces below, write the sentences from your set in one paragraph, or more.

4. Write the main idea of the paragraph(s) you wrote above.

4

Talking and Writing About Paragraphs: Main Idea

—To write well, writers must construct mental connections between and among paragraphs.

Information for the Teacher

The first part of **Talking and Writing About Paragraphs: Main Idea** involves the deliberate study of paragraph components. Then, on the basis of a given paragraph, young writers produce the main idea of the paragraph and write the next one. To analyze a paragraph in this activity, they will:

- Note the main topic or main idea
- Select a sentence that best expresses the main idea
- Write a sentence that puts the main idea in their own words

These three steps engage students in the paragraph and make them clearly familiar with it.

The next part of the activity reads: "Write what might be the next paragraph." There are at least three reasons why young writers routinely write a credible paragraph in response to that cue.

1. They have already identified the main idea in the given paragraph.
2. They have already written something associated with the paragraph.
3. Supplying students with the first paragraph gives them a running start on completing their own paragraphs; they do not have to invent a paragraph as much as continue an established idea.

Objective

Young writers will analyze paragraphs to identify main ideas, and then write paragraphs that follow directly from what they have analyzed. The result will be a seemingly automatic sense of transition from paragraph to paragraph.

Talking and Writing About Paragraphs: Main Idea

Conducting the Lesson

1. **Write a paragraph on the board or transparency.** Ask students to read the paragraph silently. Pause for the reading.

   Example: Harold moved quickly through the rides at the park. "Look at me, Mother. Watch me ride this swing," called Harold. "Mother, watch me over here. I'll bet I can ride the merry-go-round faster than anyone. Mother. Watch me ride on this swing," called Harold.

2. **Ask a volunteer to read the paragraph aloud, then ask students to identify the main idea.**

It is important to make sure that oral readings are good language models.

   Example: "Now, think about main idea. What do you think is the main idea of the paragraph?" (It's about the boy on the playground trying to get his mother to watch him play on the equipment; he's playing and trying to make sure his mother thinks he's really good.)

3. **Ask students to identify the sentence that expresses the main idea best.**

   Example: "Now, try this question. If the main idea is Harold trying to make sure his mother is impressed, which sentence in the paragraph is the one that tells the main idea?" (The second sentence.) "Read it for us." (**"Look at me, Mother."**) "Does anyone else have a different sentence that you think best expresses the main idea?" (It might be the one where he says, **"Mother, watch me over here."** He is still trying to get his mother to see him just like the sentence that Fredo had.) "So the sentence that best expresses the main idea of the paragraph could be either one?" (Fredo says his is better than the second one because it's earlier in the paragraph.)

Read the paragraph and determine the main idea. Write what might be the next paragraph.

Talking and Writing About Paragraphs: Main Idea

4. **Review main idea and topic sentences.** Remind students that the topic sentence is one that best expresses the main idea.

   Example: "Does the main idea sentence have to be early in a paragraph?" (No, but sometimes it's the first sentence. It's called the topic sentence.) "So, which one is the topic sentence, Harold?" (It's the second one because that's the best topic sentence.) "It seems as though two sentences could be topic sentences in that paragraph."

5. **Have students rewrite the main idea sentence in their own words to better express the main idea.** Pause. Listen to several main ideas or topic sentences.

   Example: "In your own words, write what you think would be the best topic sentence. Someone read what you think would be a good main idea sentence, or topic sentence." (I think the paragraph should start with a sentence like, **Harold wanted to make his mother proud, so when they went to the park, he tried to get her to watch him.**) "What did some of the rest of you write as a main idea sentence or topic sentence? Tyrone?" (I think it should say, **"Look at me, Mother," he said as he tried to get her to watch him.**)

6. **Based on the given paragraph and the established main idea, instruct students to think of and write in their own words a paragraph of three sentences or more that would follow.** Pause for the thinking and give them one minute to write the first sentence of the new paragraph.

The first session with this activity should take about 10-15 minutes, depending on how many young writers read their writings.

Example: "What do you think could be the main idea of the next paragraph? Think about that for a few seconds. What might be the first sentence of the next paragraph? You have one minute to write that sentence. Just for today, make sure this paragraph has at least three. You can make a longer paragraph, but it can't be shorter than three sentences."

7. **Instruct students to listen for main ideas as the student paragraphs are read aloud.**

   Example: ("You be careful," his mother said to him. But it was too late because Harold was making the merry-go-round go really fast. His mother got scared because she thought Harold might skip off and get hurt. But he held on tight so when the merry-go-round slowed down, he was still on, and he was okay.)

   "I'll bet that we could all write the main idea in that paragraph and then compare our idea with the writer's main idea. Read again." [The student reads.] "Write what you think the main idea is. Let's hear some main ideas."

8. **After listening to several main idea statements, ask the student writer how the statements fit with what he/she thinks is the main idea.**

   Example: "How did those statements fit with what you think is the main idea of your paragraph?" (My main idea is that Harold made his mother scared, but he didn't fall, and everyone's main idea said that, too.)

9. **On the following day, show a paragraph on the overhead and proceed with a similar main idea discussion.** There should be several of these sessions in a row to establish the thinking about main ideas, main idea sentences, and double-paragraph transitions.

Talking and Writing About Paragraphs: Main Idea

 Daily Writing Activities

The format for this lesson remains essentially as described above from day to day. As students gain experience in the process, direct them to notice that main ideas work in paragraphs and related paragraphs, much as they do in sentences and related sentences. The idea of progressively escalating main ideas is a concept within students' grasp.

Use a new paragraph every time you conduct this lesson. Prepare an overhead transparency from the children's handwritten manuscripts. This provides not only a sense of authenticity, but helps students realize that what they write is of sufficient quality to lead the instruction.

Content-area textbooks offer another important source of paragraphs. Consider the possibilities for conversation and writing in the following paragraph from a social studies book:

> **Credit for making the steamboat a success goes to inventor Robert Fulton. He launched the Clermont, the first commercially successful steamboat, on the Hudson River in 1807. Soon steamboats were puffing along U.S. rivers and lakes.**

This paragraph is filled with information, and students must understand the content before they can launch into more writing. Remember, however, they are studying and having conversation about the content. As part of the conversation, they might collect more information from social studies sources, and that might be used to write more.

Student-written directions for accomplishing given tasks provide another source of paragraphs for this activity. The first three sentences of directions for roasting a turkey can be arranged to make an opening paragraph. The questions to prompt this paragraph writing are: What is the main idea of the next paragraph? What is the first sentence in the next paragraph? What does the next paragraph look like when it is finished?

Talking and Writing About Paragraphs: Main Idea

Across the Curriculum

To apply this lesson to a social studies unit, ask, Who was this Sir Francis Drake? How do we find out more about him? What was the Spanish Armada? Where is the Caribbean Sea? How could he be a naval captain for the British, and a pirate? Direct the conversation and writing over a day or two, after collecting and organizing information. Students must do research before they can speculate on what information the next paragraph should include. Focus on the main idea of the selected paragraphs, but also on content, itself.

Example: "I have a paragraph for you to read and talk about:

> **Sir Francis Drake was a British sailor and pirate. He became a very popular hero to the British people following his successful naval battles against Spanish ships and settlements in the Caribbean Sea in the late 1500s. He sailed around the world, and he was one of the main naval captains in the British victory over the Spanish Armada.**

"Writers must know what they are writing about. They don't necessarily have to know this before they begin to write, but they have to know pretty quickly. We already know something about Sir Francis Drake, but we don't know enough to write more. To start, I need two students to collect information about the Caribbean Sea."

English Language Learners

For this activity, the emphasis is on understanding content and main idea. Language is as much a cultural matter in a school as in a Spanish-speaking community in New York. There is good reason, therefore, to make an issue of content when talking about second language learning.

Model paragraphs can focus on cultural and historic attributes of the cultures in the classroom. The pace allows for collecting, recording, and sharing information. In this lesson, there is collaborative conversation before there is individual writing, and even the writing can be conducted collaboratively.

Language Activity Sheet

Talking and Writing About Paragraphs: Main Idea

A rabbit chose just that moment to run across the road. The dogs saw it bound in front of them. They had seen lots of rabbits, but this one caught their attention like none before. They turned toward the woods in pursuit. All I could do was run after them. I didn't want any of the dogs to get lost.

1. Write the topic or main idea of the paragraph.

____

____

____

____

2. Select the sentence that you think best presents the main idea of the paragraph.

____

____

____

3. Write one sentence in your own words that you think best presents the main idea of the paragraph.

4. Write what you think might be the main idea of the next paragraph.

5. Write what might be the next paragraph.

5 Analyzing Paragraphs: Enhancing the Main Idea

—Various kinds of sentences elaborate on, or texture, the main idea; however, the main idea, not the sentences, makes the paragraph.

 Information for the Teacher

In previous lessons, young writers learned that a paragraph has a main idea and may contain a topic sentence to express that idea. They may have also written some paragraphs. However, many of these young writers still cannot write what they think their teachers would call a good paragraph, on purpose and every time.

This lesson is about paragraph writing and the ways various kinds of sentences function in paragraphs. In the following activities, students will identify various kinds of sentences in model paragraphs, write such sentences, and eventually understand why they are important.

The five kinds of sentences in this activity are examples of *elaborations*. Students should understand that all five need not appear in every paragraph. They should also understand that perfectly fine paragraphs can contain none of these kinds of sentences. This is not a formula for writing sentences that will make a paragraph, but an opportunity for young writers to notice how certain kinds of sentences can be used to elaborate on the main idea.

Five Kinds of Paragraph Sentences

1. **Main Idea Sentence:** Usually called the topic sentence, a paragraph can have a main idea without a single sentence to express it. If there is one, it can appear early, in the middle, or at the end of a paragraph. It best expresses the main idea.

2. **Clarification Sentence:** Often, this sentence follows a topic sentence that expresses an especially complex or relatively new main idea. A paragraph might open, for instance, with the following sentence: **In our study of simple machines, it is important for us to understand how the screw and the inclined plane are related.**

   A *clarification sentence* such as this might follow to clarify the first: **If you cut a piece of paper into a triangle that looks like an inclined plane, then wrap the paper around a pencil, the edge of the paper would look like a screw as the paper winds up the pencil shaft.**

3. **Example Sentence:** In a sentence describing a character, the main idea is that the woman is old, but determined: **The years had piled up on her, but she would not stop her relentless walk through the snow.**

Analyzing Paragraphs: Enhancing the Main Idea

A second sentence offers an *example* of the main idea in the first sentence: **She had to stop with every step and lift her leg out of the snow with her arms, but she kept going.**

4. **Expansion Sentence:** In a paragraph about a small pocket of wilderness near the big city, two sentences read as follows: **There calmly stood two small deer. They were munching on some grass not two feet from the edge of the highway.** An example of the calm of this wilderness is written in the first sentence. The second sentence expands on the image in the first sentence.

5. **Comparison Sentence:** In a paragraph about breeds of dogs, a sentence about the size of the German Shepherd is followed by: **If he were all gray, he would look similar to the timber wolf except that the wolf's snout is longer and more pointed.** This sentence compares the sizes of the dog and wolf, then contrasts the shapes of their faces.

There are many possible kinds of sentences young writers might use to elaborate on their main ideas in paragraphs. The five listed and explained above offer possibilities for conversation and practice.

Objective

Young writers will notice several kinds of paragraph sentences that elaborate on or provide texture for main ideas. They will write such sentences in the context of a main idea and then write whole paragraphs that contain these kinds of sentences.

Given a model paragraph, which sentence best presents the main idea, clarifies the main idea, gives examples of the main idea, expands on the main idea, and/or compares something with the main idea? Write what might be the next paragraph.

Analyzing Paragraphs: Enhancing the Main Idea

 Conducting the Lesson

1. **Begin by introducing students to the idea of elaboration.** Use an interactive activity involving a few students at a time, explaining that the activity will be repeated on different days until every student has an opportunity to participate.

   Example: "I have three objects in this box. Put your hand in the box, feel the objects. Name one object from the box." (It's a sock.) "How do you know it's a sock?" (It's soft, and I could tell by the shape.) "What shape?" (It goes in a curve so it will go up your leg.) "What's it made out of?" (Some kind of cloth, maybe cotton.) "Color?" (I can't see it. I don't know what color it is.)

   "We practice with elaboration when we work on creative thinking skills. The sock is the main idea; the other things are elaborations on the main idea. The elaborations put texture on the idea of sock. That's what we do when we use elaboration sentences in paragraphs. We give readers a chance to almost feel the main idea."

2. **On the board or overhead projector, write a paragraph that contains several of the sentences described on pages 34 and 35.** Ask volunteers to identify the main idea and the different types of sentences within the paragraph.

   Example: As he passed the small road marker way out in the woods, the man first noticed how far he was from the city where he usually worked. There stood two small deer. They were munching on some tender grass not two feet from the edge of the roadway. How beautiful it is, he thought, that there were still some places where wildlife can be safe from the bustle of the big city.

   "Read the paragraph I have on the board." (A students reads.) "Tell me the main idea of that paragraph." (It's about the man feeling good about there being a safe place for the deer.) "Which sentence, if any of them, do you think best tells about, or expresses, the main idea?" (I think it's the last one.)

3. **Explain to students how the various sentences in the paragraph support or expand the main idea.**

   Example: "If the last sentence best expresses the main idea, what do the first three sentences do in the paragraph?" (They're details.) "What kinds of details? Is there a sentence in the paragraph, for example, that expands on the main idea." (If the main idea is that there's a safe place for the deer, then the sentence about them eating grass right at the edge of the highway brings the main idea alive. It kind of makes us see the thing about a safe place for wildlife.) "It expands on the safety?" (Yes.)

"That's a kind of paragraph sentence. In many paragraphs, a sentence or two brings the main idea alive. They're special detail sentences. They expand the main idea, make it even bigger than the topic sentence does. With that sentence, we can almost see the main idea in action."

4. **Direct students' attention to the comparison sentence within the paragraph.**

   Example: "Is there a sentence that compares the main idea with anything?" (It's the last one. It has the safe place and the cars in the city in the same sentence.) "But we already agreed that would be the topic sentence. Maybe that sentence can be both a topic sentence and a comparison sentence. What do you think?" (Sure.) "So, we have a possible topic sentence that can be a detail sentence, too. There are all kinds of sentences possible in paragraphs. Sometimes a sentence can do several things at once."

5. **Ask students to reread the paragraph and, based on its main idea, think of a paragraph that might come before it.**

   Example: "Before we go to recess, read the paragraph on the board again and notice the main idea. Does everyone have a main idea? Now, think of what might be the main idea of a paragraph that comes right before the one on the board." (It's that a man was driving in the country because he wanted to get away from the pressures of his work.) "If that's the main idea of the paragraph right before the one on the board, could you write that new paragraph?" (Sure.) "All right, then write the first paragraph."

At first, writing a previous paragraph might be too complex for some students. In this case, explain again. Ask students who finish early to read their paragraph aloud. These paragraphs will serve as models for the other students.

Analyzing Paragraphs: Enhancing the Main Idea

6. **On subsequent days, write new paragraphs on the board or overhead transparency.** Review talking about sentences that elaborate by expansion, and begin a conversation about a new kind of sentence. Select a model paragraph that contains a relatively clear example of the sentence under consideration. For several days, review the various kinds of elaborative sentences, each time causing the children to write a whole paragraph. Remind them to practice by writing one or more of those kinds of sentences in their paragraph.

Put examples of the various kinds of sentences on charts around the room, not for the children to emulate or copy, but as something to notice as they write and as you conference with them about their writing.

 Daily Writing Activities

Reading model paragraphs aloud daily is the best way to support this lesson. Given that there was no need to have every kind of sentence represented in every model paragraph, nearly any source can be used for models.

Clarification sentences tend to appear heavily in science and mathematics books. Children's writing features a good representation of examples and even sentences that expand on main idea. Comparison sentences tend to appear in content books such as social studies and science. Of course teachers can also take sentences from their own writing.

Analyzing Paragraphs: Enhancing the Main Idea

 Across the Curriculum

Content area textbooks are often hard for children to read because they contain enormous amounts of data. The solution to that problem is not content-free textbooks. The reading at the beginning of this activity sets the stage for the careful reading required in content area textbooks. Deliberate attention is given to various kinds of sentences and to how those sentences work in a particular paragraph.

Example: Using material in a social studies text about the economic causes of the American Civil War, arrange the class into groups of three and assign one paragraph to each group. Direct the groups to characterize each sentence in the paragraph, then to speak with the whole class about the main idea of the paragraph, the kinds of sentences included, and, when necessary, how their sentences can be rewritten to make the paragraph clearer.

More youngsters will understand the material presented this way than by reading it and answering the questions at the end of the chapter. They will develop a sense of the kinds of sentences that appear in various texts. Repeat the activity using the science and literature book, and students will notice various sentence patterns in each. Over time, they can learn to read content-dense material more carefully and to understand how various kinds of texts are constructed.

Analyzing Paragraphs: Enhancing the Main Idea

 English Language Learners

For this lesson, the task is to identify and write various kinds of sentences. Children trying to do all of this work in a new language has the language problem on top of the sentence variety problem. In addition, their experience may not allow them to relate to the content. This issue can be addressed by beginning with ideas that can be experientially grasped.

Using short fiction helps children understand the variety of sentences that elaborate on the main idea in paragraphs. Writing a story is not unlike writing directions. In both genres, the writer tries to get readers to understand or see something. Begin a single paragraph in which the main idea is **drawing a square** and the first sentence reads: **It is not hard to draw a square if you follow some simple directions.** Every sentence that follows will also be a direction.

Think of a similar opening sentence for a paragraph in which the main idea is a character: **She entered the room and every head turned toward the door.** Ask students, "Why did the heads turn? What was there about her that made the heads turn?" The student answers can be turned into example and expansion sentences.

Language Activity Sheet

Analyzing Paragraphs: Enhancing the Main Idea

The rain continued to fall. We could see all of the cars out of our window high above the city. They were all moving very slowly, and they all had their windshield wipers on. Rain water was splashing from the many deep puddles on the streets, and the gutters were full of water running swiftly toward the sewer openings. It looked very nasty out there, but we felt snug in our hotel room.

1. Write the sentence that you think best expresses the main idea of the paragraph in the box.

___

___

2. Write the first five words of the sentence that you think clarifies the main idea.

___

___

3. Write the first four words of the sentence that you think gives examples of the main idea.

___

___

4. Write the first three words of the sentence that you think expands the main idea.

___

___

5. If there is a sentence that compares the main idea with something else, write it in the space.

____

____

6. Write what might be the next paragraph. Use at least one sentence that either clarifies the main idea, or gives examples of the main idea, or compares your main idea with something else.

____

____

____

____

____

7. Write what you think is the main idea of your paragraph.

____

____

6

A Paragraph A Day: Writing Paragraphs to Main Ideas

—Practice doesn't make perfect; practice makes permanent.

Information for the Teacher

A Paragraph a Day: Writing Paragraphs to Main Ideas is the typical paragraph-writing activity for elementary and middle-school students. It can satisfy the critical need for practice as homework and independent writing.

Practice is the key here. Several attributes of good practice are absolutely critical for the desired positive effect:

1. **Learners should practice only what they know how to do properly.** In the early stages of writing, students who write well and practice frequently become better at writing well. On the other hand, students who do not write well become increasingly accomplished at not writing well. Before releasing young writers to practice paragraph(s) daily on a largely independent basis, it is important to make sure they are writing them properly. It is likely, therefore, that they will be released to more advanced writing projects at different times.
2. **Learners should practice frequently and in great quantity.** Young writers can write more than they think they can and far more than their teachers expect.
3. **In writing, it is quality practice that produces mastery.** Young writers become better mostly because of what they do under teacher direction.

If this lesson occurs on the basis of these three principles, students will become better writers, and the writing behaviors we are trying to establish will become automatic. ***Automatic*** is the key word here. Young writers must become sufficiently practiced so they can find paragraph patterns in their own writing quickly and effectively. They must become sufficiently practiced to begin a main idea, notice its development through several sentences, and notice its closure—all while paying attention, not to the paragraph, but to the development of a larger piece of writing.

Objective

Young writers will write several paragraphs every day, to achieve familiarity with thinking and writing in paragraphs and with arranging their writing into paragraphs. **Note:** While writing daily paragraphs will increase the probability of a measure of automaticity for fourth- and fifth-graders, this objective may not be fully achieved by every child. Nevertheless, the pursuit is important, just as arithmetic practice is important, even though all children may not become automatic in arithmetic at the fourth- and fifth-grade levels.

A Paragraph A Day: Writing Paragraphs to Main Ideas

Conducting the Lesson

1. **Initiate a paragraph writing activity, specifying a main idea.** Explain to students that their completed paragraph will be their ticket to recess. Remind them to include a main idea in each paragraph.

   Example: "Think of a paragraph in which the main idea is a time when you did something that made someone feel good. Think of what that paragraph might look like." [Pause.] (**Last night I carried the groceries for my grandmother when we went to her house to help her get ready for a party she is having for her friends.**) "What's the first sentence in your paragraph?" (**My grandmother is having a party.**)

   "When it's time for recess, I am going to be standing at the door. A paragraph, in which the main idea is something you have done for someone that made them feel good, will be your ticket out the door. How will I know if you have written a paragraph?" (It has a main idea in it.) "So when you write the paragraph, make sure it has a main idea."

2. **Take five minutes or less to make a check in the grade book for every "ticket" that comes in.** Do not read all the papers. Students need the practice more than anything else. Return the papers to the Ticket-to-Recess box after recess.

There's a rule of thumb about the teacher's reading load in a writing program: *If young writers write as much as they must in order to learn to write well, no teacher can read it all; if a teacher can read it all, young writers aren't writing enough to learn to write well.*

3. **The following day, announce another ticket to recess.** Direct students to write a paragraph in which the main idea is something they know how to do. Use the same process described above.

4. **On that same day, have students write a paragraph with another specified idea.**

   Example: "As your ticket to afternoon recess, write a paragraph in which the main idea is a time you had to learn something that was hard, but you learned it because you worked hard on it."

Write a paragraph in which the main idea is a time when you tried to help someone.

5. **Direct students to write two paragraphs in addition to their other writing assignments.**

6. **On the third day, assign tickets to both morning and afternoon recesses.** Then 10 minutes before it is time to go home, assign a third paragraph for homework as a ticket to get back in the room the following day.

Call attention to how much students are writing, and reinforce their good work.

7. **On the fourth day, assign tickets to both recesses.**

8. **Assign a paragraph for homework, this time having students write the paragraph, plus the main idea of the paragraph that might follow.**

9. **Debrief.** At the end of the week, recall the number and kinds of paragraphs students wrote.

   Example: "Yesterday, you wrote four paragraphs. For homework you wrote a paragraph and the main idea of the next paragraph. Now we could write four paragraphs a day, but I don't want you to work that hard. Next week, on Monday and Wednesday only, we will write only three. We'll see what the week after that looks like."

10. **Conduct the activity for several weeks, planning so students write at least five paragraphs every week.** At this rate, after six weeks, each student will have written at least 30 paragraphs.

As you read student work, provide the feedback that helps refine their practice. Routinely ask them to read their paragraphs aloud, modeling for the other students.

A Paragraph A Day: Writing Paragraphs to Main Ideas

Daily Writing Activities

Listed below are main ideas for writing a paragraph a day:

1. Something that makes you laugh
2. A trip you remember well
3. A truck loaded with oranges speeding down a mountain road
4. An explanation of how a light bulb works
5. Some interesting mail you received
6. A lost puppy (Also write what might be the main idea of the following paragraph.)
7. A description of your bedroom
8. A female character in a story (The paragraph will be a character description. Write what you think might be the next paragraph.)
9. A time when you received a great telephone call
10. Something you did to help one or both of your parents
11. Something you learned recently in social studies
12. Something you learned recently in science
13. A major news story in the newspaper and/or on television recently
14. Something you do very well
15. Something you know about a country or culture other than the one in which you are living
16. A good time you had at a holiday celebration
17. A terrific meal you had while you were on vacation
18. A great time you had while being with friends
19. A plan you have for what you would like to do when you are an adult
20. Something you think you know that almost no one else in the class knows. (This does not mean a secret of some sort. It is just something you know about or how to do.)

A Paragraph A Day: Writing Paragraphs to Main Ideas

 Across the Curriculum

The applications for using this lesson across the curriculum are clear. The paragraph-a-day is cued the same way every time: **Write a paragraph in which the main idea is ...**

In a unit on weather, for example, the paragraph cues may read: **Write a paragraph in which the main idea is the difference between cumulus and cirrus clouds.** After reading and discussing the material about the weather patterns that produce such clouds, the cue may be: **Write a paragraph in which the main idea is the weather pattern that produces cirrus clouds.**

Most students can keep up this pace, even when applied to the content areas. But for a few the pace may be too strenuous. This is not a call for a reduction in the pace for the entire class, but rather that a slower pace for a few students might be more appropriate.

 English Language Learners

Begin with the fact that in all languages, paragraphs are defined by their main ideas. Young writers for whom English is not yet a comfortable language may benefit from writing their paragraph-a-day in their more comfortable language. As the weeks pass, make adjustments. For example, of the five paragraphs written by students in the fourth week, at least one can be in English. The fact that the teacher does not speak or read the child's native language should never preclude the child from writing in it.

The ability to speak a native language other than English need not be a handicap in school. It is a disadvantage only when it is treated as a handicap. The mission is to help everyone master the language of the larger community, but that in no way precludes students from using their native language for learning.

Language Activity Sheet

A Paragraph A Day: Writing Paragraphs to Main Ideas

Note to Teacher: To eliminate the daily responsibility for starting the tasks, put the cues on task cards or sheets and store them in a box at the classroom writing center. Each morning, post a sign displaying the number of paragraphs for the day and/or the schedule.

For example:

Wednesday: Tickets for morning and afternoon recess and one for homework.

Thursday: Tickets for morning and afternoon recess, one before art class, and one for homework.

The task cards, may be designed as shown below:

- Write a paragraph in which the main idea is **something you have learned recently about the balance of power in the United States Constitution.**

- Write a paragraph in which the main idea is **something you have learned recently about the role of James Madison in writing the United States Constitution.**

- Write a paragraph in which the main idea is **an interesting fact you have learned recently about Abigal Adams.** Write the next paragraph so that the main idea is **an interesting fact you have learned about Dolly Madison**.

- Write a paragraph in which the main idea is **a description of an interesting setting for a short story.**

- Write a paragraph in which the main idea is **something about the great San Francisco earthquake.**

- Write a paragraph in which the main idea is **something you learned recently about the Makah Tribe of people.**

- Write a paragraph in which the main idea is **something about rainforests in the northern hemisphere.**

- Write a paragraph in which the main idea is **a necessary characteristic of a good friend.**

- Write a paragraph in which the main idea is **one of the advantages of being able to speak and read two languages.**

Writing a Story: Story Grammar

—A grammar for short fiction is nothing more than a way to show how a story can be constructed.

 Information for the Teacher

Writing a Story: Story Grammar helps young writers learn to write short fiction and become aware of the characteristics of stories. We need to understand several points about short fiction and story grammar.

1. A grammar is a taxonomy, a codification, of something. There are taxonomies, or grammars, for all kinds of things: biology, language, and the earth's evolution, to name but three. The Periodic Table of Elements that hangs in chemistry classrooms is a taxonomy or a grammar of chemistry. It presents some basic properties of construction in chemistry.

   But the Periodic Table of Elements is not chemistry. Knowing the Periodic Table does not mean one can do chemistry. It is merely a way of explaining something about chemistry.

2. There is a grammar for stories. The story grammar in this lesson consists of four elements:
   - A story must have a character or characters.
   - A story takes place somewhere. This is called the setting or the environment. The setting gives the story a context; it gives the characters a place to be characters.
   - The story has to be about something, and that's called the problem. How a character deals with or solves the problem compels readers.
   - A story has a resolution. The ending shows how that character solved the problem.

3. Knowing about the elements or a grammar for chemistry and language does not mean that one can use it to construct language or practice chemistry. However, it is useful for understanding how the language and chemistry has been constructed.

4. Knowing a story grammar does not mean one can write a story, but it does help ensure that all the critical elements of a story have been included.

 Objective

Young writers will compose stories on the basis of story elements that they brainstorm.

Writing a Story: Story Grammar

Conducting the Lesson

1. **Begin story writing by directing students to brainstorm elements that will appear in the story.** Write one example on the board, then list good student examples on the left side of the board.

   Example: "We're going to begin story writing by making some lists. Let's make a list of short character descriptions. I'll give you an example (old man), and then I'll need six or eight more."

2. **Next, direct students to volunteer short descriptions of names of places.** Explain that these will be story settings. Write one example on the board (forest), and list student examples to the right of the list of characters.

   Example: "Next, let's make a list of places where stories can take place. These are called story settings. Let's make a list of short descriptions."

3. **Explain to students the role story problems play in the story.** Write one example on the board (a lost pet), then ask students to volunteer short descriptions of story problems and their resolutions.

   Example: "Every story is about something, usually a problem the character(s) must solve. These are called story problems. They're what the plot is about. I need a list of problems or obstacles."

   "Stories end when the problem is solved, or at least understood, and is no longer such a big obstacle. These resolutions make up the story ending. Now, give me a list of resolutions."

There should now be four lists of about eight to ten items each. Notice that all items on the lists, except for the first ones offered by the teacher, came from the children.

Arrange one item from each of four elements of a story grammar into a short story.

4. **Direct students to pick one item from each list, and without writing it down to, hold those four items in their heads.**
5. **Explain that the four items in their heads represent the main parts of their story.** As an example, model a simple story around four items. Then ask students to think of (but not write down) stories using their own four items. After several students tell their stories, explain that these are the beginnings of a short story.

   Example: "Everyone has a character, a setting, a problem, and a resolution. I selected **the ten-year-old girl**, **the farmhouse**, **no friends**, and **fun at Sunday School**. Now, it's time to think of a story. My story will be about a little girl who lives on a farm. Because she lives so far from town, she doesn't have a chance to make friends at parties and after-school activities, so she's lonely. Her mother and father are very concerned because they want her to be happy. They arrange to have a special Sunday School program at the church in the country and invite the city children to attend. Many do come, and the farm girl becomes friends with several of the boys and girls from town. Now write down the story in your mind."
6. **Put students in groups of two to four.** Ask them to tell their stories to each other before they begin writing.

If 15 minutes is too much time to keep everyone occupied, cut it to 5 or 10 minutes.

7. **After students orally share their stories with each other, give them about 10-15 minutes to start writing stories in two or three paragraphs.** After 15 minutes, call time.
8. **Ask students to share their written story starts aloud and place them in their writing folders.**

These sharings often provide exemplary models for other students. The whole idea of this first session is to create a start. Youngsters need lots of starts. Much of the creativity occurs as writers invent the core of the story. The rest of the task is to flesh out that start.

9. **The next day, ask students to select four different items from the lists, and give them 15 minutes to start another story.**

10. **For the next three consecutive days, direct students to return to their folders and find one story start to work on for 15 or 20 minutes.**

11. **On Monday of the following week, create new lists, and establish a new story start.** On Tuesday, make still another start, and on Wednesday another. On Thursday, direct students to work on an unfinished piece of writing from their folders.

12. **On Monday and Tuesday of the third week, make a new list and a new story start.** On Wednesday, announce that they will have three days to work in their folder and to turn in a finished story.

13. **On Wednesday, conduct conferences with students.** Ask the following questions to help them reflect on their stories: What are you trying to do in this story? Where are you now? What do you have to do next to move your story along?

Make suggestions in the conferences, but try not to turn students from what they say they are trying to do. The story belongs to the mind of the writer. The teacher's guidance is useful and legitimate, but only in the context of students' plans.

14. **On Friday, collect any stories that are complete.** If only a few students are not quite finished, tell them you want the stories by Monday.

15. **During the first several days of the fourth week, read through the stories.** A good story has a plausible story line, character(s) that fit the problem and seem to belong in the setting, and a resolution that seems logical. It should engage the reader or appear that it will engage students. Write comments about how the story works and about the various kinds of mechanical problems (e.g., use of conventions, spelling) that need attention.

16. **Think of several instructional groups that might need to be formed (writing dialogue, punctuating dialogue, paragraphing with dialogue, plausibility in stories, and so forth).** When you return the papers, tell students to read what you have written on their papers, and then to put the stories back in their folders to work on later.

In time, students should have as many as a dozen stories in various stages of completion and should be working on them at least several times every week. One point of this lesson is to get the children to create a lot of material to work on and to have the time and guidance for that work.

Daily Writing Activities

The daily activities to support this lesson should be based on the children's lists. In cooperative groups, they can make their own lists and exchange them. However, there might be some merit in occasionally providing a list. The following are examples of four lists that can be mixed and matched:

Characters	Settings	Problems	Resolutions
animals pet lover man in a wheelchair Primus, a robot	city street the roof dirt road tropical island	challenge lost bird raining car accident	winning gracefully gaining a friend check in the mail robots take over
sleeping grandmother ants in a line Indian man carpenter	parking garage small restaurant desert road room with cage	robot revolt fell down hungry war	smoke alarm works memory comes back a door opens people gather to help
archeologist criminal old woman walking cowboys	barn dark night fields on a cold day camping outside	a threat a dare child is sick unfairness	they win the game invitation for dinner good sleep getting satisfaction
hikers family members baseball team puppy	mountain side church lawn party farm in the winter supermarket	storm car won't start lost cow something smells	call from home graduation day freedom return home
two young wolves two good friends well-dressed woman executive	an elementary school a snowy hillside an apple orchard grassy field	no electricity an argument liar hungry	they shake hands moose vacation graduate

Writing a Story: Story Grammar

 Across the Curriculum

Grammar is the word used in linguistics to describe the list of rules for how language is constructed and used. Dictionary definitions and references in thesauruses associate it with language study. However, the root meaning of the word is "a set of rules."

In good story writing, the characters, settings, problems, and resolutions are connected in some plausible way. Discuss with students other areas where a set of rules or conventions describes elements and how they work. In chemistry, elements are associated in certain ways to create compounds. Taxonomies exist in biology, as well. Are there rules or conventions for how the primary colors are used to create greens and pinks? Are there rules or conventions are there for how guitar strings are strummed to create certain chords?

Returning to language study, introduce fourth- and fifth-graders to phonology. There are 46 phonemes and each one has a symbol. With those symbols displayed on a chart in front of the room, they can do a phonemic transcription of a paragraph or two from one of their stories. In a story exchange around the room, young writers can engage readers with the challenge of reading in an especially interesting part of the story in phonemic code.

English Language Learners

This activity supports the recommendation of Peregoy and Boyle (*Reading, Writing, and Learning in ESL*, Longman, 1992) regarding the use of story mapping to help youngsters understand story structure for both reading and writing. In the reading program, read a simple story and ask the children to build a map of the story based on the following skeleton.

Someone→	Want→	But→	So
the pigs	strong houses to be safe	the wolf blows down all but one house	the pigs boil the wolf and live happily ever after

In response to hearing, reading, and talking about "The Three Little Pigs," a group of fourth-graders developed the story skeleton above. As children learn to analyze their storybooks and develop the skill and insight to look at other writer's stories in a structural perspective, they are more likely to think structurally about their own stories. This sense of how stories are constructed also aids in reading comprehension.

Language Activity Sheet

Writing A Story: Story Grammar

Make a list of four characters here	Make a list of four settings here	Make a list of four problems here	Make a list of four solutions here
________	________	________	________
________	________	________	________
________	________	________	________
________	________	________	________

1. Find a partner and exchange Language Activity Sheets. From this sheet of four lists, select one item from each list and, without writing anything for one full minute, think of how those four items could make a story. Write the story idea in the space below.

   ____

2. Now think of how to elaborate on a basic story idea so the characters take shape. Give your character a personality. Who is this character? What does this character do? Like? Dislike?

   ____

   ____

   ____

3. It is time to think about the setting. Why are the character and the action in the story in that setting? Write something that will make the connection between the setting and everything else is the story. Make the reader see it, hear it, or smell it.

____

____

____

____

4. Write the first few lines of the story in the spaces below. Then don't write anything more on the story until tomorrow. Give the story some time to live in your mind. Write the rest of the story tomorrow and the next day.

____

____

____

____

8 Writing a Story: Inventing Your Own Starter

—The fundamental creativity in fiction writing occurs as the writer invents the core around which the story will be woven.

 Information for the Teacher

Traditional story starters, whether commercially developed or teacher-made, that provide young writers with the story line, preempt inventive creativity. Given certain cues, young writers can invent their own story starters. This lesson gives the opportunity for creativity back to young writers.

In his thriller, *Misery* (New American Library, 1994), Stephen King refers to "falling through a hole in the paper," which describes a writer so immersed in the story that all sense of his surroundings disappears. This kind of immersion tends to happen when writers work on their own inventions.

There is no way to predict how many youngsters, or which ones, will get beyond the first several sentences in this lesson on any given day. Conduct the activities at least twice every week until everyone eventually invents a story starter.

 Objective

Over time, all young writers in the class will invent their own story line and pursue it on their own terms. This activity should produce a story from most of the children in the class at least once a month.

Writing a Story: Inventing Your Own Starter

 Conducting the Lesson

1. **Direct a story starter beginning with the name of a character, the character's age, and the name of a city or town.**

   Example: As soon as Shirley heard her mother's call, she woke up and thought of her 13th birthday.

2. **Write examples on the board, then ask students to write the first sentence of the story using the name and age of their character.** Write an example sentence on the board as students write.

   Example: "Think of the name of a story character, not one from television or a comic book, just a name. I'm going to put the name I'm using here on the board. Write yours at the top of a your paper. Now, near the name, write your character's age."

3. **Begin to write a second sentence, then turn to the class and tell them to write their second sentence and include the name of the city or town.**

   Example: It was cold in Albuquerque this time of year, so Shirley was careful not to step on the cement floor until she put her feet into the snug slippers she kept under the covers.

Don't worry about the children keeping up with you.

4. **Write the next sentence on the board or overhead, following whatever the first two sentences dictate.** Then turn to the class and tell them to write their third sentence in response to what the first two sentences tell them. "Listen to what your first two sentences tell you. Then write what you think comes next." Continue to write the example paragraph on the board or transparency.

   Example: Every time she woke up in that cold room with the cold floor, she thought about the other children in her class who had carpet on the floor where they lived. It made her sad sometimes, but then she would smell the fry bread in the kitchen and stop thinking about floors.

Name a character and time of day in a sentence, and then write the next sentence based on the idea(s) in the first sentence.

Writing a Story: Inventing Your Own Starter

5. **Continue to write consecutive sentences on the board, and, at the end of your first paragraph, announce that you will be finishing your story on the board as they write.**

   Example: "Keep going with your story now. Take it as far as it will go. I'm going to write mine up here."

6. **After the fifth or sixth sentence, direct students having difficulty writing a story to stop and work on unfinished writing, instead.** Remind them that this is writing time, so everyone must write, if not on today's activity, then on something from their portfolio.

The portfolio is each student's repository of works in progress, false starts, scraps of paper with ideas scribbled on them, and pieces in need of revision. Whenever a student makes a choice not to work on the piece set up for the day, (s)he must return to the portfolio and work on something else.

7. **With 15 minutes left in the session, approach a student who appears to be in the midst of a pause, and conduct brief individual conferences of no more than two minutes.** Ask the student a series of focus questions about the story such as, What are you trying to do here? What is your story about? Where are you now? What do you think you have to do to accomplish what you are trying to do in your story?

Conduct as many as three or four conferences of this sort during the 15 minutes. Assure each writer that there will be time in class to work further on the story, but there is no reason why they should not work on it independently at home.

8. **After 15 minutes, call time, and announce to students that when they want to continue writing their story later that day, they must put a "Do Not Disturb" sign on their desk while they write.**

Out of 30 students, there may be five so into their writing that they don't want to be disturbed and 25 more just playing the game. This is normal. It is unreasonable to expect everyone to identify with any one instructional activity.

9. **In the afternoon or on the following morning, conduct a new activity, directing students to name a character different from the one they wrote about the last time.** Again, they name a city or town, but this time instead of an age, name a time of day. Have them write the first sentence, then the second, the third, and continue as described above.

10. **During the last five minutes, conduct conferences with three to five young writers.**

If some students are having trouble with this writing, allow them to use the remaining time for writing on other projects in their portfolio. Those who want to return to their morning story may do so, as long as they first write what could be done with the character, town/city, and time of day that they just started.

11. **Construct a third session, beginning with a different character's name, a setting (place) of their choice, and an ailment suffered by the character.** Continue conferencing with students.

12. **For the fourth session, begin with the name of a location or setting (an elementary school, supermarket, city council meeting, birthday party, old shack in the woods, gas station, and so forth).** Invent a character that belongs in that setting. Give the character an age that is appropriate to the setting. Include in the first sentence the character's name and the name of the place.

13. **Continue as above through the seventh session.** During the second week, conduct only three of these sessions, then two each week for a month.

That will make as many as 18 sessions. In those 18 sessions, every child in the room will "take off" at least once and probably as many as three or four times. Even if it's only once, the young writer who experiences it will, perhaps for the first time, know what it feels like to "fall through the hole in the paper" (p. 66).

Writing a Story: Inventing Your Own Starter

 Daily Writing Activities

Session One: Setting, Character, Time of Day

Session Two: Character (Child, Male), Setting (Outdoors), Animal

Session Three: Character (Child, Female), Setting (A room in a house), Time of Day

Session Four: Character, Local Neighborhood, A Pet

Session Five: Adult Character, Setting, Traveling

Session Six: Character (Ethnicity different from the writer), School, Grade Level

Most story starters include a prompt for a character. However, it is possible for a story to begin on the basis of a setting alone. A ferryboat, for example, may have a destination on the other side of the river where people cross every day. The people and the reasons for crossing can be the story line.

Notice that the story starters do not contain a story problem. To provide the story problem is similar to the preemptive story starter we are trying to avoid with this activity. As soon as you say, "A boy sees a friend cheating on a test, now write a story," you have established the story line for the young writers, and the rest is merely filling in the blanks. Instead, give young writers character and setting possibilities and let them learn to run.

 Across the Curriculum

Consider the following example of using sentences from a story related to a social studies unit. The excerpts can be written on the board or projected from transparencies. A follow-up activity will test the student's recollection of the unit and provide paragraph writing practice based on the procedures described in this lesson.

Example: "Here are the opening two sentences for a story about someone we have been reading about:"

> **Biting wind cut through the thin blanket that Joseph had wrapped over his shoulders. He was large, so the blanket didn't reach past the tops of his knee-length moccasins.**

(It's Chief Joseph.) "Yes it is, and you now have the first two lines in the story. Remember, fiction has to be believable. That means your setting descriptions have to be accurate. Where are we going to put this story?" (Idaho, Washington, and Oregon.) "Right. And Joseph has to be accurate, too. I need a group of three to write this story." [Select three students.] "Look at this one."

> **Fifteen young men sat around the fire, even though the weather outside the crowded cave was blistering hot. They sat silently, naked to the waist, cloth bands around their foreheads, waiting for their leader to speak.**

(Is it Manuelito?) "Yes, tell us what you remember." (He was the Navajo man who escaped from Kit Carson and hid in Canyon de Chelly. "I need three writers for a Manuelito story." [Select three students to write the story.]

 English Language Learners

We first used **Inventing Your Own Starter** in a seventh-grade class where every student was a native speaker of Spanish, and 16 of the 20 in the class were in transition from ESL classes to English only classes. It was stunning how easily and quickly six of those young writers took off with the first story. Most of the rest of the class wrote as much as a paragraph in response to the first set-up. After five set-ups over four days, all but two seventh-graders wrote at least one story.

Within a few months, we used the activity in classrooms with students as young as third-graders. **Inventing Your Own Starter** offers a realistic opportunity for young writers learning English to bring their own experiences to the story-writing task. Of course, there is no reason at all why their fiction writings cannot be written in languages other than English.

Language Activity Sheet

Writing a Story: Inventing Your Own Starter

"Where is your laboratory?" the news reporter asked the white-haired man.

"Here," he answered, gazing into the reporter's eyes. "Here," he said as he pointed to his head.

The reporter laughed. "Okay, Dr. Einstein. You got me there. Then how about showing me where you keep your scientific apparatus, the stuff you use to experiment with."

Albert Einstein rolled his eyes impatiently. He looked at the reporter as though he had asked one of the world's dumbest questions. Then he reached into his pocket and pulled out a fountain pen. "This, my friend, is my apparatus. This is what I use to record my thinking."

1. Write at least five things you know to be true about Albert Einstein.

____

____

____

____

2. If you were going to write a story in which Albert Einstein were the main character, name at least two settings or locations where the story could be placed.

____

____

____

3. If the story were about Albert Einstein between his birth and the age of 20, what would be the main story line?

____

____

4. If the story were about Albert Einstein, but didn't emphasize science, what might the story be about?

____

____

5. In an accurate story about Albert Einstein, there would have to be other characters from his life and time. Write the names of at least three people whom he knew well or with whom he worked.

____

____

6. With two collaborators, write a story in which Albert Einstein is the main character. Remember, you must be accurate in your *factual* description of Einstein and his work. The fiction is in what you, and the other writers, do with the facts.

9 Writing Reports of Information in Four Parts

—The more reports young writers write, the more they practice writing reports. If they are to become good at it, they must write many good ones.

 Information for the Teacher

Writing Reports of Information in Four Parts is more rule-bound than its counterpart, **Writing Reports of Information as Exploration** (page 86). These kinds of reports give young writers something specific to count on; the information is always collected the same way, and the writing always appears in the same format.

Part 1. Problem or Question: The problem or question must be stated clearly and precisely. All terms must be defined.

Part 2. Procedures: The procedures should state exactly what was done to solve the problem or answer the question.

Part 3. Results or Findings: This is the solution to the problem. There is no editorial comment in this part. This is only the evidence.

Part 4. Conclusions: Here the writer has a chance to discuss the research and make comments about the findings. The writer might also suggest future research related to the question.

To become accomplished at report writing, it is in young writers' best interest to write many reports. The more reports they write, the more they practice. A 1000-word report is one instance of practice. Four 250-word reports provide four chances to practice. And if young writers write ten reports of 100 words, they practice report writing ten times. The four-part report is short and can be applied to any curricular area and to any demand for report writing.

 Objective

Fourth- and fifth-graders will write reports of information that reflect the classic scientific report four-part form.

Conducting the Lesson

1. **Explain that together the class will be writing a report. List the four parts of a Report of Information (see page 66) on the board or overhead transparency.**

2. **Announce a problem statement for the focus of the report.** Write this question on the board or transparency.

   Example: "First, we have to begin with a problem statement or question and define some terms. Maybe a question is a better place to start. Let's work with this one: Can girls with light hair do more push ups than girls with dark hair?"

3. **Select a student to be the recorder for the day, then explain Part 2 of a Report of Information in Four Parts. Define the terms in the proposed problem statement.** Remind the student recorder to write down the problem statement and the definitions of terms.

   Example: "Let's define some terms. What is a push up? We have to know exactly what we are talking about. We must decide where the hands have to be. Is it a push up if the hands are together right under the shoulders, or do they have to be far apart? We must decide if the back has to be straight and if the nose has to touch the ground."

4. **Lead a discussion about how the problem will be tested for a solution.** Explain the idea of sampling and averages. Remind the recorder to make notes on the discussion.

   Example: "We will count all the push ups the girls can do all day Wednesday. Recorder, please make a note that there will be one person who counts for each person who does push ups, and one person to determine if each push up is a real one. There are 11 girls in the room, and only four have dark hair. If all of the dark-haired girls do the push ups, which four light-haired girls get to do them?"

5. **Conduct the experiment.** Have the recorder do any calculations and record all the results.

How do we find out if fourth-grade girls with light hair can do more push ups than fourth-grade girls with dark hair?

6. **Assist the class in drawing a conclusion.**

   Example: "The difference between the dark-haired and the light-haired girls is less than one push up. What does that mean? (Less than one on the average.) Does that mean that dark-haired girls are stronger? Remember, the question is about being stronger." (No, it doesn't mean one is stronger because it wasn't even a whole push up difference for each girl.)

7. **Ask the recorder to read the problem statement or question to the class.** As the recorder reads, write it on the board. Direct the recorder to read the definitions and procedures. Write those in narrative form on the board, each under their own header, Question and Procedures. Then direct the recorder to read the results. Write the results in narrative form under the header, Results. Then write the header, Conclusions.

   Example: "What do you think we learned about hair color and push ups from this experiment?" (They don't matter.) "Write a sentence about the results being inconclusive."

8. **Draw the student's attention to the report on the board.**

   Example: "Look at the board, boys and girls. That's a Report of Information in Four Parts. This kind of report is outlined in four parts." [Point out the four parts.] "It's how scientists report their observations. We set up an experiment and recorded our observations. Tomorrow, we'll try another question."

The push up example is effective because it produces enough curiosity to generate several more experiments and written reports. The children are involved, and they discover that variables such as hair color are irrelevant to push ups.

9. **Set up a different sort of report on the second day, but follow essentially the same procedures.** Write the name of a person unfamiliar to students and ask them how they might go about finding out who the person is.

   Example: [W.E.B. DuBois.] "Who is this? How would we find out who this is? How would we find out why (s)he is important? (Can I go to the library?) "Why? What are you going to look for?" (To look in the card catalog.) "That only works if he/she wrote something that we have in our school library, but that's a good idea."

Write the procedures on the board, and make students be specific about how they will follow them .

Similarly, when a student suggests conducting an interview, ask, "With whom? Make a list of everyone you think you should interview." Students will soon have a list of procedures that will lead them to identify the person.

10. **Remind students to report the results in the third part of the report.** After this, they write a conclusion sentence or two about the importance or influence of the person.

11. **On another day, pose a new cue for a research question and record student answers on the board.** If an interesting research question is not volunteered, pose one for them.

    Example: "What is there to know about Pennsylvania? Why is Pennsylvania called Alabama's sister state? Where could we find information on these questions?"

If fourth- and fifth-graders write as many as two Reports of Information in Four Parts each month of the school year, that is 18 reports for each young writer, or a teacher reading load of 540 Reports of Information in a class of 30. That doesn't count, of course, the stories, letters, autobiographical incidents, and opinions they are writing.

If they wrote those genres on the same schedule as the four-part reports, the reading load would be 2160 papers in 36 weeks (4 genres x 18 instances x 30 writers), or 60 papers a week. It's not reasonable to think that teachers can, or should, read them all.

We recommend approximating the following rule of thumb: *Every young writer should have something read and reviewed by the teacher every week.* That means one piece of writing, and not necessarily the whole piece. The purpose is to write and receive constructive feedback from the teacher.

Writing Reports of Information in Four Parts

 Daily Writing Activities

Follow the procedures on the previous pages with a wide variety of possible questions. While the problems and questions below may not appear all that unique, the idea is to focus on procedures and writing that displays scientific thinking in four parts (see p. 78).

The following topics can be used as the focus of four-part reports:

1. Any of the fifty states in the United States
2. The nations represented in the United Nations, those not represented, and/or why they are not represented
3. Presidents of the United States or any contemporary leader in the world
4. Various writers, artists, and athletes
5. Occupations
6. Local issues and problems (e.g., What will happen if the city's antiquated sewer system is not upgraded?)
7. Will a seven-inch No. 2 wooden lead pencil make a longer line than a seven-inch No. 2.5 wooden lead pencil?
8. Will a lima bean grow more quickly if placed in the soil with the "button" up or down?
9. Will sunlight make a bean grow better than a light bulb will?
10. Is body weight a variable in running fast?
11. Are fourth-grade reading books harder to read, or easier, than fifth-grade reading books?
12. Do people remember real words longer than nonsense words?

 Across the Curriculum

The daily examples show clearly the implications for cross-curricular writing. For example, in the area of music, Reports of Information in Four Parts can lead young writers into biographical study. There is a rich musical heritage in the United States, fed by influences from all over the world. Begin with Scott Joplin. Listen to his music. Conduct the research that will lead to information about who he was, what he wrote, when he wrote, and how his music influenced the music that followed.

 English Language Learners

As there is generally more than one musical heritage in most elementary school classrooms across the United States, consider posing questions such as, How is the music of Latin American and Caribbean peoples both alike and different? and, How does the traditional music of Japan differ from that of China?

This activity provides students with opportunities to learn about various composers, the sounds of their music, the lives they lived, and where they lived. Reports of Information in Four Parts can serve as the musical foundation of the year for fourth- and fifth-graders.

Language Activity Sheet

Writing Reports of Information in Four Parts

Part 1. The Problem or Question:

____

____

____

____

Definitions of Terms (as necessary):

____

____

____

____

____

Part 2. Procedures:

____

____

____

____

Part 3. Findings or Results:

____

____

____

____

____

____

____

____

Part 4. Conclusions:

____

____

____

____

____

____

____

____

10 Writing Reports of Information as Exploration

—When writers write what they care about, they come to understand more about what they write.

 Information for the Teacher

Writing Reports of Information as exploration is a very different process from **Writing Reports of Information in Four Parts**. It is exploration, much as four-part research is exploration, but the writing comes out very differently. Such a report can take multiple twists and turns as the writer discovers the topic and makes it increasingly clear.

In this type of report, the exploration itself is reflected in the writing. It is impossible for the writer or the teacher to know the length, organizational structure, number of references, or the outcome. In a Report of Information in Four Parts, the experiment or research is described in an objective manner, with the reader an observer of what is being reported. By comparison, a Report as Exploration engages the reader as the experiment or research unfolds.

An Information Report in Four Parts begins with a question or problem which is likely to read something like this: "The purpose of this research is to describe the travels of Marco Polo." By comparison, a Report as Exploration will begin somewhat differently, with a question such as, "Have you ever wondered about the man whose name you call in the swimming pool hide-and-seek game, Marco Polo?" Although the report as exploration reveals the travels of Marco Polo and much of the same information revealed in a four-part report, it also allows writers to explore as they learn.

The beginning paragraph or sentence of a four-part report often reveals the thesis. In an exploratory essay, the writer's motive is far different. The exploratory report is about learning while writing, and the thesis is very likely to appear at the end.

Young writers will identify a topic of interest to them and write a report or essay on that topic. The report will be informative and organized in a logical manner. However, it will be written as a narrative and will not necessarily adhere to the traditional research report format.

Writing Reports of Information as Exploration

Conducting the Lesson

1. **Pose six to ten brainstorming cues in a row to which students will respond.** Response time for each list should not exceed one minute.

   Example:

   1. Things that make you laugh
   2. Things that make you cry
   3. Things that you would like to learn more about
   4. Things that make you angry
   5. Things that you love
   6. Things that you like to read about
   7. Things that are long
   8. Things that you have learned from watching television
   9. Things that you are trying to learn but are having a difficult time learning
   10. Things that you do well
   11. Things that you could teach someone else to do
   12. Jobs you think you would like to do when you're grown

2. **Assist students in identifying a topic to explore.**

   Example: "Is there an idea or two on your lists that you care about, something you would like to know more about or something that strikes your interest? What do you have on your list that you're trying to learn and having a hard time with?" (Second base is hard because you have to know which way to go on every play, and you're in the middle of the infield all the time. That's what I want to know right now. And I put long division and playing my trumpet on there, too.)

Learn as much as you can about Marco Polo from writing about his life and travels.

3. **Assist students in thinking of what they want to know about their topics.**

   Example: "How are you going to find out more about the best second basemen?" (Look it up.) "Where?" (In an encyclopedia?) "Which one?" (I don't know.) "If your coach tells you that Robbie Alomar is the best second baseman playing today, what will you write about Robbie Alomar?" (I have to find out who he is.) "I have a suggestion. You need at least two players playing right now and two from ten years ago. Several books on our bookshelf might have some of that information. They're called almanacs and are filled with information."

4. **Continue to answer students' specific questions until most understand the assignment.**

   Example: (How long does it have to be?) "A report is about as big as your topic. If you have a tiny question, you might have a short report. If the question is big, the report might be big. It's impossible to tell you how long a report should be. Think about making your report interesting. Fill it with information that is interesting to you, and it will probably be interesting to your readers."

5. **Remind students about the importance of citing references in this kind of report.**

   Example: (Do we have to have a bibliography?) "References tell readers where the information came from, so if you have any information, you must tell where you found it."

Remember, for many students this is a new kind of assignment. Whatever previous experience they have is probably anchored in curriculum objectives that explicitly dictate the format and process.

In an initial session like the one described in this lesson, about half the class will find their way to topics or questions that can occupy their research and writing time for several days. The rest may require some small-group or individual attention. After a day or two, most of the children will identify something they care about.

6. **On the second day, conference with students.** For those students already working on something, provide resources, ideas, and reflection by asking probing questions:

   What are you trying to accomplish here? What is this about? What is your purpose? What will you be helping your readers to know and understand? What have you accomplished so far? Where are you in the process? What have you done? How do you think you will organize the report?

What do you have to do yet? How much more do you have to do? What information do you need that you haven't found yet? When do you think you'll be ready to write the report? What do you think the report will look like?

Such questions are more for eliciting student thinking than for eliciting specific answers. The conferences are meant to help young researchers and writers step back and think about what they are trying to do, what they've done, and what they have yet to do.

7. **Conduct Power Writing sessions with students who have not found a direction when the third session begins.** Ask them to write as much as they can as well as they can in response to one or more of the topics they select from your lists. Tell them to write until they run out of ideas on a topic. If they want to remain with that topic but need to know more, encourage them to begin researching. If they do not want to remain with that topic, tell them they are free to change topics as soon as they have written at least 50 words.
8. **On the third day, conference again with students and encourage them to move ahead.** At the end of the third session, most students will have started writing and will have the entire fourth and fifth sessions to complete their work.
9. **Schedule a "Knowledge Faire" at the end of the week during which each student may deliver a brief oral report based on his/her research.**

The Knowledge Faire will last no longer than 40 minutes, so everyone in the class may not have an opportunity to share the first time. Assure students that they will have another opportunity to share at another Faire in a week or two.

10. **Ask students to submit their reports for your review and evaluation.** The grading rubric below involves assigning 25 possible points for each report:
    - 10 points for an organizational structure that clearly presents the information
    - 10 points for thoroughness and accuracy of content/information
    - 5 points for mechanical control

As students become increasingly familiar with the rubric by using it to evaluate their own work and to give feedback to one another, student editorial boards can evaluate half of the reports for each Knowledge Faire. Credit students for doing the work, but do not read every report every time. Merely spot-check them to make sure the rubric is being applied with some degree of reliability.

Writing Reports of Information as Exploration

 Daily Writing Activities

There are five daily activities associated with this process. Day One is the set-up. Days Two, Three, and Four are for writing. Then, on Day Five, students give the oral reports in the Knowledge Faire.

We have learned that young writers tend to be compelled by their own learning. This is especially the case when students discover they can use the activity to learn and report on what they are interested in. After the first few reports, therefore, many students will need only a reminder that they will be doing an exploration report that week.

Some youngsters will need help setting up every time. The Monday set-up is always the same. It consists of six to 10 brainstorming cues like those described in the first procedure in this lesson (e.g., make a list of things that come in threes, make a list of green things that are flat, make a list of pink things that are fluffy.) In each series of cues, include two or three that focus on what students would like to know more about, what they already know how to do, and what interests them.

You may hear young researchers ask if they can continue what they were working on the last time. Given the opportunity, some youngsters might want to work on the same topic the entire year. Explain that if they work on the same topic, they must research it from a different perspective.

Example 1: "Certainly you may work on the same topic, but each time you look at the topic you have to look at it a little differently. For example, you may work on horses again, but you already researched different breeds. This time learn about the origins of the draft horses, the Clydesdale, and so forth."

Example 2: "The last time you worked on horses. This time write about another work animal."

Writing Reports of Information as Exploration

 Across the Curriculum

After several week-long sessions of personal interest research and writing, conduct the set-up in a particular content area. For mathematics, make a list of occupations that use geometry, places where you see geometric shapes and solids. The research and writing in this case are not necessarily about the geometry, but geometry is the catalyst. For example, a list of places with geometric solids may include Egypt where there are pyramids, the ball park where there are spheres, and a toy store where there are cubes (blocks). The research and writing might focus on Egypt, pharaohs, sand, the Middle East, mummification, or the difference between pyramids and tetrahedrons.

 English Language Learners

This research and reporting is especially applicable to the range of diversity found in classrooms. The procedures described in this lesson utilize the rich variety of student experiences represented in the classroom as a curricular focus. All languages can be used for the writing, and even for the research, if the resources are available. Then, if English is common to all the youngsters, the oral reports can be prepared and delivered in English, making the activity an authentically bilingual experience for each youngster in the room.

Language Activity Sheet

Writing Reports of Information as Exploration

1. Make a list of things you can do with Jell-O.

____

____

2. Make a list of the best books you have read.

____

____

3. Make a list of the four most interesting jobs or occupations you know about.

____

____

4. Make a list of four things you know about a one dollar bill.

____

____

5. Count the number of times the numeral 1 or the word one appears on a dollar bill.

6. What is a mint? What are the dimensions of a dollar bill? Whose picture is on a five, a ten, a fifty, a one hundred dollar bill? What is a Federal Reserve Note? What is a Silver Certificate? What is scrip?

____

____

7. What are the three most interesting things on this sheet so far? Put a circle around the most interesting thing you've listed above.

______________ ______________ ______________

8. If the item inside your circle in Number 7 were a research and writing topic, what do you think you would need to learn about it? Make a list of four things:

__________ __________ __________ __________

9. Name someone you could call to learn about a topic on this sheet.______________

Name someone you know whom you could interview to learn more about a topic on this sheet.

____

Name a place you could go to find people who might know about a topic on this sheet.

____

10. Decide on a topic or question for your research this week. Today (Monday) you must name a topic. On Tuesday and Wednesday you will conduct your research. On Thursday and Friday you will write your report. Then on Friday afternoon, you will share your research with the rest of the class. Your topic is

____.

11. Make notes from your research on another sheet of paper, if necessary.

11 Power Writing: Drafting for Revision

—Fluency is critical in learning to write; no one learns to write without putting black on white.

Information for the Teacher

Telling young writers to write a rough draft doesn't necessarily guarantee that they will produce one. Many 10-year-olds think this merely means to write something sloppily and then revise by recopying it with better handwriting.

Power Writing is a fluency lesson designed to encourage students to produce multiple rough drafts for revision. Essentially, fluency is about quantity, not quality, with quantity measured by the number of words the children write. Therefore, this lesson is not about the number of words they spell correctly or have in effective sentences. For this lesson, the more words students write, the more fluent they are.

Because the primary criterion in **Power Writing** is fluency, or quantity, young writers focused on getting black on white end up with numerous rough drafts to revise.

Objective

Young writers will write as much as they can as well as they can in response to a cue they select from among two or three. They will then revise a rough draft and discuss their revisions. Finally, students will deliberately practice the variety of revision possibilities discussed.

Power Writing: Drafting for Revision

Conducting the Lesson

1. **On the first day, introduce Power Writing to students by putting two words on the board and asking them to select one word as a writing topic.** Direct them to write, in one minute, as much as they can, as well as they can, about their topic.

   Example: "Here are the words. " [Write ***cup*** and ***book*** on the board.] "Choose one for your topic. Use that idea as your topic. Write as much as you can as well as you can in one minute. Ready. Go!"

At this prompt, most children will begin to write immediately. Several will hesitate. Some who begin right away will write a sentence or two and stop. One or two youngsters may write a list of words. As soon as they find out that the word count is nearly always higher when they write in sentences than in lists, they will write sentences.

2. **During the one-minute writing time, place on the board or overhead transparency a Power Writing chart, like the one shown on the Language Activity Sheet on p. 101.**

3. **When one minute is up, call time.** Tell students that they must stop immediately after they finish writing about the word they're on. Ask them to count their words and write the number in a circle at the top of their paper.

4. **Beginning with 0-5 words, ask students to raise their hands when they hear the number of words they wrote called out.** Count the raised hands and write the number of raised hands on the Power Writing chart. Continue up the chart until no raised hands are left.

   Example: "Raise your hand when I call the number that matches the number of words you wrote. How many wrote between zero and five words? Now, I want to see the hands of everyone who wrote between six and 10 words."

Pick a word. Use it as the idea for writing as much as you can as well as you can. After three Power Writing rounds, select a writing from either Round Two or Round Three to revise.

5. **Conduct Rounds Two and Three with different pairs of words.** Remind youngsters that they will have one minute to write as much as they can, as well as they can, on the topic they choose.

With three rounds recorded, each column will show a slight or even dramatic change upward. Direct students' attention to the columns. Many will notice that their numbers increased in Rounds Two and Three. If the children count wrong or occasionally raise their hand for a number higher than the one they actually wrote, it's irrelevant. The objective, writing for fluency, has been met. This introduction to Power Writing takes about 15 minutes.

6. **On the second day, do three new rounds of Power Writing.** When students have written to three cues and for three rounds of Power Writing, they will have three new pieces of writing, with the number of words in each one recorded on the chart.

The numbers are likely to rise again with each round. They may be even higher than the previous day. The children's focus will be on their numbers, and that's just fine because this is about fluency. This is also an excellent opportunity for young writers to have genuine rough drafts to revise.

7. **The second day is revision day.** Begin the revision portion of the activity by directing students to select a piece to revise.

   Example: "I want you to select a writing from one of the rounds you wrote today. Select either Round Two or Round Three, not Round One. I want you to choose one of your last two rounds because by then you were warmed up."

8. **After students choose a writing, let them know they have two minutes to work on it to make it better.** Tell them that they have two minutes for revision because revision always takes longer than drafting. It's not necessary to tell students what revision means or how to do it. Simply let them know they are to work on their writing so they can turn it in for a grade, or to make it the best they can. Set the stop watch, and give them the signal to start.

9. **After one and a half minutes, announce that there is only a half-minute left.** At two minutes, ask them to finish the sentence they're working on. After about 15 more seconds pass, call time.

Power Writing: Drafting for Revision

10. **Ask students to focus on their revisions.** Ask them what they did to their writing. As they volunteer kinds of revision and editing behaviors, write them on the board.

    Example: "Legibility, spelling, and punctuation in writing are critical for your audience. People have to be able to read what you have written. What else did you do when you revised your Power Writing?" (I had to finish it.) "What do you mean by 'finish it?'" (I put in sentences at the end to finish it. It wasn't done.) "So you wrote more to finish the thought for your readers." (Yes.)

11. **Continue adding to the list until students have no more revision strategies to report.**

As the year moves along, students will add to the list until you have a student-produced list of the critical revision strategies. Typically, fourth- and fifth-grade lists include items such as:

Capitalization	Punctuation
Spelling	Add a beginning
Add an ending	Rewrite one or more sentences
Add detail	Legibility
Change the order of sentences	Change words

Revision is an enormously complex part of writing which even the most accomplished writers find difficult and sometimes avoid altogether by hiring others to do it for them. By allowing young writers to discover and discuss their own revision processes, they will gain an increasing repertoire of strategies to call upon.

Power Writing: Drafting for Revision

12. **As students add to their list of revision strategies, ask them to share the ways they applied them to their writing.**

    Example: "You said you changed the order of your sentences." (Two sentences had to be turned around.) "How did you know that?" (I read it and they just seemed to be in the wrong order. It sounded better if I changed them.) "Read those two sentences as you have them now." (**There were millions of them all over the West. But they were killed when the railroad came through.**) "How did you have it at first?" (It was the other way. I wrote that when the railroad came through they were killed. Then I wrote the sentence that says there were millions of them.) "It sounds as though it would work either way." (Yes, but it's just better the way I changed it.)

13. **Work through the list of revision strategies, explaining that the students will use each other's strategies to make their writing better.**

    Example: "We're going to practice some of the revision strategies we discuss in this class. Take a careful look at the piece you just revised and study the order of your sentences. See if you can find a place where your piece would work better if the order of two or more sentences were changed. I'll give you a minute to look."

    "Did anyone make any changes?" (I changed two sentences.) "Read what you had before you changed it." (I wrote about baking. I said that you have to put the filling in a pie pan, and then I said you have to put the crust in the bottom of the pan.) "And you changed those?" (Yes. You have to put the crust down first, and then you put the filling in.) "Why didn't you write them in that order in your rough draft?" (Maybe because I was writing so fast. But when I went back and looked to see if everything made sense, it didn't.)

14. **Students should work with one or more of the revision skills from the list each day of the week.**

Every session of Power Writing produces drafts for revision. Over the course of a school year, fourth- and fifth-graders can practice revision skills at least twice each week, establishing a twice-weekly revision program. After several weeks of this, the master list of revision skills from their own experience can be put on a wall chart. This chart is organic, developed by students and expanded through the efforts of the class.

Power Writing: Drafting for Revision

Daily Writing Activities

Daily activities for this lesson center on the three pairs of words used for the three rounds of Power Writing. Once children realize how the cues are used, they'll eagerly volunteer words to create a bank of cues for future use. The objective is fluency, so young writers try to accumulate higher and higher numbers.

Of course, they will eventually encounter a ceiling, or limit, based on their individual psycho-motor capabilities. The ceiling varies somewhat by individual, but the teacher and students will know when they've reached a plateau. They will also become aware of the fact that the cue itself contributes to the level of fluency on any given round (e.g., a student may be more fluent on the topic of **MTV** than on **democracy**).

Notice that this is a very different drafting/revising interaction than what typically happens when young writers have the time they need to draft as well as they can, and then cannot find anything to revise. There is always something to revise in this activity. Furthermore, the drafting/revision interaction in Power Writing reinforces both quantity **and** quality. It is very different from attempts to get young writers to think of their draft as inadequate so they have something to fix. Power Writing is much closer to what many experienced writers do when they write.

Power Writing: Drafting for Revision

 Across the Curriculum

Power Writing works with words from any area of the curriculum. Use ***plane, pulley, inclined plane, lever,*** and ***fulcrum*** as cues. Use ***fraction, decimal, ordinal, mean, mode,*** and ***median***. Use ***peninsula, island, inlet, continent, arid,*** and ***temperate***.

 English Language Learners

It is critical for children working in transition from ESL or bilingual programs or Sheltered Instruction to have the freedom to use language under circumstances that reflect competence in their native language, the new language, and/or combinations of the two. They need comprehensible directions and experienced achievement. The latter can be ensured by using cues designed to reflect prior knowledge. Adjust the Power Writing chart into increments of two or three instead of four to five to give them a sense of progress. Encouraging children to also use the language they are most comfortable with assures them that words in languages other than English are valuable.

Language Activity Sheet
Power Writing: Drafting for Revision

Power Writing Chart

My Daily Fluency Record

Date		Round One	Round Two	Round Three	My Average
	66-70				
	61-65				
	56-60				
	51-55				
	46-50				
	41-45				
	36-40				
	31-35				
	26-30				
	21-25				
	16-20				
	11-15				
	6-10				
	0-5				

12 The Autobiographical Incident

—Autobiographical incidents aren't about using young writers' prior knowledge; they are young writers' prior knowledge.

Information for the Teacher

It could be argued that autobiographical writing is the most important literary genre. Accomplished writers routinely report that they write for themselves. Hemingway, for example, said he wrote for two audiences, himself and someone he loved. Autobiographical writing seems to satisfy writers' needs to record their thoughts, feelings, and experiences.

Teachers can promote and support writing about autobiographical incidents by framing cues and guiding students' thinking. As in any other type of writing (reports of information, persuasion, fiction), certain rhetorical elements are present in autobiographical writing:

- Autobiographical writing is about recording one's own experiences.
- Prior knowledge isn't the avenue to content, it *is* the content.
- Young writers are their own audiences. (This does not mean, however, that they will write whatever they want and keep it private. It means that they are writing about the most important topic in their lives: themselves.)

The question of evaluating autobiographical incident writings is a critical one. It's absurd for a teacher to say to a student, "You had a 'C' experience." At the same time, it is important to persist in an expectation of excellence. When a student is not writing up to his/her capability, take a moment to assign a revision of the piece in question. Remind students that good writers always write as well as they can under the circumstances offered.

Objective

Teachers will guide young writers in using their own experiences as topics or cues for autobiographical writing.

The Autobiographical Incident

Conducting the Lesson

1. **Introduce autobiographical writing by directing students to take out a piece of paper and get ready to write.** Start by asking them to put a number **1** on the top line. Announce that they will be listing items from one to six down the left side of their papers and will need to leave several spaces between each item.

   Example: "Think of a celebration, a birthday, a special meal or feast, a holiday, something special that happens in your church, a family get-together. Beside the number **1** on your paper, write the name of this celebration."

2. **Guide students in recalling specific details of the event, or celebration, and in writing them down on the list.**

   Example: "Write a number **2** on the next line, and list the names of the people who were at your celebration. You don't have to name everyone, but you should name at least those most important to you. Beside number **3**, write a phrase or sentence about something that happened at the celebration. Beside the number **4**, write a phrase or sentence that tells about two more things that happened at the celebration. Beside number **5**, write a word, a phrase, or a sentence about the kinds of feelings you associate or connect with that celebration. Beside your number **6**, write a word, a phrase, or a sentence about anything you associate with the celebration that you haven't written yet."

Pause between prompts for the thinking and writing.

3. **Direct students to review their list about the event or celebration and decide what they think is the most important idea about it.**

   Example: "Now, you have lots of notes about your celebration. Go over what you have written, and find what you think is the most important idea about this incident. Put a circle around that item or idea."

4. **Direct students to examine the list for an item that summarizes the event or celebration.**

   Example: "Find an item or idea that you think could be used to summarize, or end, a writing about your celebration. Put a star [*] at the beginning of that item or idea."

Think of a time when ...Who was there? What was the time of day? Year? What feelings do you associate with that time?

The Autobiographical Incident

5. **Tell students they will have 15 minutes to write their autobiographical incident using items from their lists.** Remind them that as the writers, they can use any of the items on the list in any order and things that aren't in their notes at all.

6. **Announce that they will have as much time to write as they need, but that they will be interrupted in 15 minutes for some conversation before they go on.** Let them know that although they will be invited to share, they will not be required to read their writings aloud.

Teachers always have the responsibility to monitor student work. The issue here is how to monitor autobiographical writing. Below are some procedures to consider:

1. Before reading a particular piece or posting writings in the writing center, announce *before students begin writing* that you will be reading their work.
2. Reserve some time for private writing. Tell students, "I will not read this one unless you ask me to."
3. Direct students to put their autobiographical pieces in a special section of their portfolio. Tell them, "I'm going to read in the autobiographical section of your portfolio. Put a star [*] at the top of any pages that are open for my reading. Put a paper clip on any page(s) that you do not want me to read. I will read two pages that you open to me, and I will not read any page with a paper clip on it."
4. Make sure students are doing the writing. Give gentle reminders to those who are not doing the writing and credit to those who complete the assignments.

Important Note to Teachers: In autobiographical writing, there is always the chance that a child will write something that must be addressed. For example, a student may write about being afraid of a parent because a sibling's arm was broken in a recent beating. This must be reported to someone, the nurse, principal, or department chair.

After taking the child aside to check the accuracy of the story, explain as carefully as possible what will take place and why you must follow through. The child may feel betrayed; however, the chief concern of the teacher must always be the safety of the child.

The Autobiographical Incident

Daily Writing Activities

We recommend that students be guided through autobiographical thinking and writing once a week, or at least every other week. During a 36-week school year, the result at this rate will be approximately 18-30 autobiographical incidents. The writings that students consider their best one or two over the year, can be bound in a booklet, titled *All About Us* and donated to the class library.

1. This is something I know how to do.
2. I'm not frightened very often, but this is something that scares me.
3. I remember a time when I did something that made a friend feel good.
4. I remember a time when I learned that someone was a good friend.
5. This was my very best birthday.
6. I get all dressed up for this celebration in my community.
7. This was the very best piece of mail I have ever received.
8. I remember my best summer.
9. I went on a trip once, and I'll never forget it.
10. I can name the best teacher I have ever had, and I can tell why (s)he was best.
11. This is my favorite room in my house.
12. This is my favorite holiday.
13. This is about something I am still trying to learn.
14. This is my greatest accomplishment.
15. I was most proud of myself when ...

 Across the Curriculum

A useful application of autobiographical writing occurs when young writers monitor their own learning progress. Consider making an autobiographical assignment at the beginning of an art project, for example. Ask students to keep a record of every experience they have as they make kites. Give them several minutes at the end of each art session to write. After they fly the kites, direct them to take their notes from each day, and write an autobiographical incident that covers the week.

Once young writers have written an autobiographical incident about their experience in art class, a similar assignment can be developed to accompany units on metric measurement; the properties of solids, liquids, and gases; or how to read music. Such writing makes children consciously aware of their own learning behaviors and processes, while reinforcing their learning.

 English Language Learners

Much of children's experience in school is, in a sense, artificial. So it is sometimes difficult to make classroom writing experiences relevant to children's prior knowledge and real-life experiences.

However, it is clear that the writing in this lesson is about real experiences and the way children see them. Using these procedures, some youngsters learning English as a second language are able to write autobiographical incidents of admirable quality.

Language Activity Sheet

The Autobiographical Incident

1. Think of a time when you played in a game of some sort. Write a word, a phrase, or a sentence that names that time or incident.

____

____

2. Write the names of some of the people who were there when you played the game.

____

____

3. Write a sentence that tells something that happened during the game.

____

____

4. Make some notes about one or two other things that happened during the game, right after the game, or right before the game.

____

____

5. Make a list of the feelings you had right before the game or right after the game.

____

____

6. Write a sentence that tells something special that you haven't already written about this game.

____

____

7. Put a circle around something you wrote above that seems like the most important part of your memory of the game you played.

8. Put a star (*) beside what you think could be the last thought or idea you would write if you were writing about your experience in the game.

9. Write a sentence that tells what it is about the game that makes it stand out in your memory and makes you think about it here.

____

____

10. Think about someone reading your piece about that game. Think about what you would want your reader to understand most about your experience. Write a sentence that tells what you want your reader to understand most.

____

____

11. Write what you think would be a good sentence to describe your experience playing that game.

____

____

12. On another sheet of paper write a rough draft of the autobiographical incident.

13 Your Opinions in Writing

—Opinion writing is not about having an argument, but about making an argument.

 Information for the Teacher

Opinion writing is one of the most complex kinds of writing for young writers. Research shows that elementary students seem to handle narrative writing reasonably well, but have difficulty with opinion writing. One reason for this is their lack of experience with opinion writing. Another reason is that opinion requires a relatively sophisticated level of thinking. If we teach opinion writing carefully, we can overcome both of these problems.

We can begin with several points of basic information:

- Experts in the field of writing opinion have special procedures and styles.
- In opinion writing, the writer states a position on an issue and explains the position.
- In persuasive writing, the writer states a position on an issue, explains the position, and suggests reasons why readers should agree.
- Successful opinion writing reflects the ability and willingness of the writer to think beyond "how a problem strikes me," and to consider what the problem means in its broadest sense.
- Successful persuasive writing reflects the ability and willingness of the writer to consider the implications of a problem, to enter the reader's mind, and to consider another perspective.

The intellectual ability of fourth- and fifth-graders to "decenter" and consider themselves and others at the same time doesn't automatically transfer to an ability to write opinion and persuasion. To make this leap, students must receive proper instruction. Neither the teaching nor the learning of the skill is easy, but they are both feasible. Teaching opinion and persuasion to 10- and 11-year-olds is about establishing some basic work habits associated with writing about opinions.

 Objective

Young writers will craft opinion and persuasion writings from selected prompts offered by the teacher. The extent to which young writers achieve success is based on the extent to which the writings contain the critical elements of opinion and persuasion.

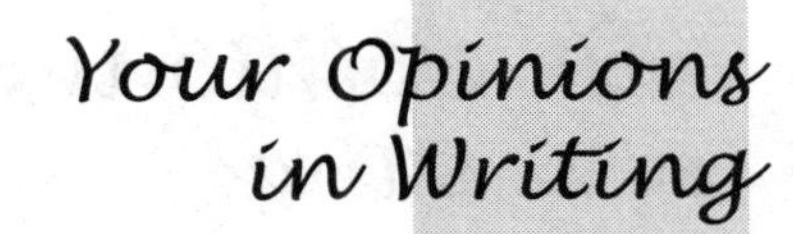

Conducting the Lesson

1. **On an overhead transparency or chalkboard, write two opinion statements.**

   Example:

   1. **There should be a dress code in all schools beginning in the third grade.**
   2. **There should be candy vending machines in elementary schools.**

2. **Ask a volunteer to read the statements aloud.** After students have a chance to react to them, conduct a general conversation to clarify and discuss the meaning and implications of each statement.

3. **Direct students to select one statement and to write it on their paper exactly as it appears on the board.** Next, ask them to decide whether they agree or disagree with it. Instruct them to write *agree* or *disagree* on the line below the statement. Pause for the writing.

   Example: "If you disagree with the idea of dress codes in school, your writing will be about why you disagree, and your reason can't be something like, 'because it's stupid.' You must think about what dress codes mean and what they might do in a school. You must think about whether a dress code means everyone must wear the same things, or whether everyone must wear certain kinds of things. You must think about whether you disagree with all dress codes, and then decide why you have made an intelligent decision to disagree."

4. **Call on the student who can usually think on the spur of the moment to model a statement of opinion.**

   Example: "Give me a good reason why you disagree with dress codes." (Because people should have the right to dress as they want to.) "Why? Is there some law about that? Police officers have to wear uniforms." (Well, I think people should have the right to dress the way they want.) "Why is that important to you?" (Because some people can't have all the clothes other people have, so it isn't fair to say they have to dress alike.) "So, write that reason down. Now, everyone, think of why you agree or disagree with the statement you selected, and write your reason." [Pause for thinking and writing.]

Given two opinions, select one, and write your opinion, the reasons for your opinion, and the reasons why a reader should think your opinion is reasonable.

5. **Call attention to the issue, the position on the issue, and the reason for the position, and explain again that these are the three parts of opinion writing.**

   Example: "You now have what we call an *issue*. That's the statement you wrote down first. You also have what we call a *position*. That's your opinion, whether you agree or disagree. And you just wrote what we call the *reason*, explaining why you either agree or disagree. It's time to write now. Your piece of writing will have those three parts."

6. **Lead the children through using the three parts to write three sentences, then explain that to finish the opinion writing, they must write a closing sentence.** Give them an example on the board.

   Example: "I might close my opinion writing with a sentence similar to this one: **That is the reason why I don't think a dress code is a good idea for children in school.**"

7. **Collect the student's papers, without their names, and post them on a Best Effort Board.** After recess, read several aloud, calling attention to the parts and how these parts help readers understand the issue and the writer's position.

Remind students that stories also have parts: character(s), setting, problem, and resolution.

8. **On another day, pose several more issues for writing about opinions.** Guide students as they organize those parts in sentences and write a closing sentence. This time, direct them to put their names on their paper and post them on the Best Effort Board.

9. **Direct as many as three opinion pieces a week for two or three weeks.** As students write their third or fourth opinion piece, suggest that they may have more than one reason for their position on an issue and that their reasons could take more than one sentence to write.

Students won't become good at opinion writing by writing only one or two. Practice is everything in writing.

10. When students have written five or six opinion pieces of four or five sentences each, give them an example of a persuasive sentence and introduce the idea of persuasive writing.

Example: "You have been writing your opinions on various issues. On the last writing someone wrote her opinion that children should not be allowed to bring refined sugar snacks to school because it's bad for their teeth. Why should I agree with her? I understand how she feels about it, but what could she say to persuade me to think her way?"

11. Direct students to write a persuasive sentence immediately following their reason sentence. Show them that the writing is now five sentences long and that one of the sentences is about persuasion, making it persuasive writing.

Example: "To make this writing persuasive, she can write a sentence such as this one right after her reason sentence: **Most cavities in children's teeth come from eating refined sugar**."

Once students have written several of these, put two statements on the board and prompt opinion or persuasive writing. Simply remind them that the first has four parts and the second has five.

Daily Writing Activities

We recommend that fourth- and fifth-graders do opinion writing as often as twice per month throughout the year. Conducting daily activities requires that the teacher provide issue statements for students to work with. The following statements work effectively in elementary classrooms. Similar statements can be based on issues common to particular schools, communities, or neighborhoods.

1. Children in school should be allowed to choose their teachers every year.
2. No one should be allowed to ride a skateboard on any public sidewalk.
3. There should be a story hour every day in our classroom.
4. The school should provide music lessons for anyone who wants them.
5. Children should bring their lunch from home so the school wouldn't have to provide school lunches.
6. Boys should have to wear shirts with collars in school.
7. Fifth-grade girls should read to first-and second-graders every day.
8. No students should be allowed to move on to the sixth grade until they have memorized the capitals of every state in the United States.

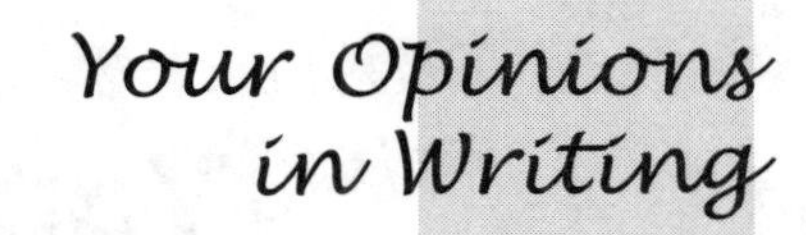

 Across the Curriculum

An example for a cross-disciplinary application of this activity is "What's Worth Knowing?" In social studies, for example, provide students with the issue statement: **The history of ancient Egypt is important in the fifth grade.**

Direct half the class to write on the basis of agreement, and half on the basis of disagreement. After the writing, pair students who agree with those who disagree for opinion sharing. Have each pair join another pair for sharing until there are two large groups sharing the importance in the fifth-grade of knowing about ancient Egypt.

This kind of writing and conversation engages learners in thinking about the value of the topic. As a variation, have children write and share "What's Worth Knowing?" writings both before beginning a unit and again after finishing it.

 English Language Learners

It is important that children whose native language is not English clearly understand the process and purpose of opinion and persuasion writing. Once they grasp the idea and form, they can handle the directions as well as anyone else. Research recommends heavily that these children work with one another on complex tasks. The complex writing tasks of opinion and persuasion fit this type of collaboration very well.

Arrange the children into groups of two or three. Ask them to write one collaborative piece based on thinking and conversation in the small group. The first and most important part of the conversation, certainly, will be to agree on their position on the issue. As they frame the essay together, one member writes as the other members dictate the ideas. Then, the group can be asked to think and write again, this time from the opposite position. Using this procedure, any issue can be discussed and written from two different perspectives.

Language Activity Sheet
Your Opinions in Writing

Choose an issue:

- **Because skateboarding is so dangerous, people should have to get a license to ride, just as they do to drive a car.**
- **It would be a good idea if fourth-and fifth-graders had a "homework buddy" at the (firehouse, retired people's home, juvenile court school) with whom they could talk on the telephone every night about doing homework.**
- **School days should be extended by two full hours.**

Part I: Write a sentence that names the issue.______________________________

____

____

Part II: Write is a sentence about your opinion on the issue. ________________

____

____

Part III: Write a sentence about the reason for your opinion on the issue.

____

____

Part IV: Write a sentence about why someone else should have an opinion similar to

yours.____

____

____

 Conducting the Lesson

1. **To introduce informal letter writing, make a cooperative arrangement with a teacher in a lower grade to begin a weekly letter exchange between students in the two classes.** Students in the higher grade will write letters that will be delivered by Wednesday. The recipients in the lower grade will read them and write an answer which will delivered by Friday of the same week.

This works well if fifth-graders work with third-graders, fourth-graders with second-graders, etc.

2. **Have students begin by writing informal letters about something associated with school.** These first letters will be short. Students will need to keep in mind that their letters will be read by students in a lower grade. Their letters must be delivered by Wednesday of that week.

3. **Repeat the process the following week.** Explain to students that while the frequency may increase if a pair chooses, it may not drop below one letter each, per week.

4. **After three weeks, develop a different cooperative arrangement with the same lower grade at a different school.** Explain to students that this new arrangement does not mean that the first letter-writing relationship must stop. It merely means that they are now writing letters to two different students every week, and receiving two, as well. Continue this second arrangement for approximately three more weeks.

This exchange involves students who have never met, so it is up to the writers to develop a relationship with the other students through their letter writing.

5. **After six weeks of such letter writing, students will accumulate at least six letters, all written to a real audience and all serving the purpose of intercommunication.**

Write a letter to the treasurer of your city and inquire about the amount of money collected from parking fines over the past year.

The value of involving younger children in this process can't be overlooked, nor can the value of writing specifically to younger writers' interests and literacy levels. If the process stopped here, it would make a considerable impact on young writers' letter-writing abilities and inclinations. But this has only been the set-up.

6. **In the seventh week, begin Monday's writing session with an announcement that the letter-writing project will change.** Tell students that they will now be writing more letters and writing to different people. Explain that they may continue to correspond with their old partners, but that if they decide to stop, they must explain why they are stopping, and their partner must know that they will remain available as a friend.
7. **Explain to students that, beginning this week, they will write two informal letters per week to friends and relatives, for as long as it takes to receive an answer in the mail, written directly to them.** Explain, also, that the letters need to be at least 80 words in length and may not say that they are part of a school project and must be answered.
8. **Purchase a box of envelopes, or ask the school to supply them.** Make arrangements to accumulate a supply of postage stamps for the letters.

If it will be difficult for parents to supply the stamps, ask the PTA, or run a bake sale. Do not purchase postage out of your own pocket.

9. **Direct students to make a list of people they know who are not their classmates.** Suggest that they include on the list relatives who live locally and out of town, old friends who have moved away, and so forth. Direct everyone to collect their addresses at home and bring them to school the next day.
10. **Ask students to select one person from their list and to write a letter to them about something that person would find interesting.** Ideally, the letters go out on Tuesday, but Wednesday will work on a two-per-week schedule.

    Example: "Think of something to write about that your person might find interesting. Remember, you are trying to communicate informally about what's going on in your life. Your friends and relatives are interested in you, so give them some information that will stir their interest and get them to write back. Remember, your letter should have at least 80 words and must not say that you need a response."

11. **Roam the room during the 10- to 15-minute writing time.** Notice what the children are writing about and how they are writing. Remind them as necessary about legibility and mechanical control. Remind them also that their letters affect impressions others have of them and of the school. If you see inappropriate content, direct them to write about something else.

12. **On Thursday, have students write a letter to another person on the list.** Ideally, these should go out on Thursday. Students should know that the more letters they send, and the better the letters are, the higher the probability they will receive an answer. Remind them that when they receive their first answer, they have completed the assignment. At that point, they need not write any more letters, but our experience tells us that they're so deep into the communications that many continue.

Two letters per week not only encourages quantity, but increases the probability of getting a response. But, if this is too much pressure, alter the plan to make it one per week.

13. **Using a similar system, immediately follow the eight weeks of informal letters with formal letters.** Students will practice writing these letters for not more than two weeks, writing perhaps two per week. Read them quickly and give feedback.

14. **Make overhead transparencies of model letters, and lead the children in conversation about what a formal letter looks like (formally blocked), what it contains (letterhead which may contain the sender's address, date, greeting, body, close, and signature), and how it's crafted (tightly organized and brief).** Point out that business letters go directly to the point, explain that point, then close.

15. **On Monday of the second week, announce that they will write two letters each week until they receive an answer or response addressed directly to them by name.** Explain that as soon as they receive a response and demonstrate the ability to write a formal letter that receives a response, the assignment is over.

16. **In the third week, ask students to prepare a letter which will be mailed on Wednesday or Thursday.** Read their letters and conference with them, giving feedback on what they've written. Students can also meet in workshop groups to read and critique each other's letters for form and effectiveness. On Wednesday they can use these suggestions to prepare another letter to mail on Thursday.

Writing Letters: Formal and Informal

 Daily Writing Activities

One way to prompt letter writing activities is by using a matrix specifying the address and subject. To start, young writers select one item from each list, find the address (family address book, newspapers, public library, telephone call, almanac, and so forth), and prepare their letters. An informal letter matrix might look like this:

Letter To	Letter About
Aunt	Thank you
Uncle	Request
Mother	I have a question ...
Father	This is why I did ...
Sister	Could you please ...
Brother	Invitation
Best Friend	What have you been doing?
Other Friend	This happened to me ...

A formal letter matrix, on the other hand might look like this:

Letter To	Letter to Person	Letter About
Auto Dealer	Sales Director	Commission rate for salespeople
City Hall	Council Person	How to get elected
City Hall	Mayor	Nature of job
State Government	Legislator	How to get elected
National Government	Executive	What is a veto
Police Department	Chief	Crime rate
Indian Tribe	Education Director	Scholarship opportunities
University	Admissions Officer	Admissions standards
Business	Human Resources Officer	Job opportunities with a company

Cues or prompts from a matrix might read as follows:

1. Write a formal letter to the sales director of a local car dealership, and inquire about the sales commission earned by salespersons.
2. Write a formal letter of inquiry to a university, and ask about their admissions standards.
3. Write a formal letter of inquiry to a reservation in New Mexico, and ask about tribal scholarship opportunities for its youth.
4. Write an informal letter to your aunt or uncle, and thank him or her for a gift you recently received.
5. Write an informal letter to one of your friends, and invite him or her to visit you at your house.

Writing Letters: Formal and Informal

 Across the Curriculum

Using this activity, students will write about seven to 10 letters in the fall. If they remain on schedule and write well enough to get responses, the letter writing sequence will consume approximately 11-12 weeks. Another seven to 10 letters again in the spring makes at least a dozen letters during the fourth-grade year. If this is repeated in the fifth grade, students will have written at least two dozen letters. This quantity will establish, for most of them, a fair measure of letter writing competence.

Consider the letter-writing possibilities in social studies, alone. There are approximately 250 tribes of indigenous peoples in the United States. All have tribal offices and will send information packets on request. Their addresses can be acquired from the National Congress of American Indians (NCAI) or the Bureau of Indian Affairs (a division of the Department of Interior, Washington, D.C.). Imagine what a social studies corner will look like if the list of tribes is divided among the children in your class and each child sends two letters. No social studies book can compete with that much up-to-date information.

 English Language Learners

Again, consider the possibilities in social studies. In every community, there are organizations that serve the needs of immigrants and families who tend to work in languages other than English. Children can write letters to find out the names and addresses of the organizations, then write letters of inquiry and receive answers in their native languages. This validates the languages and the fact that they serve communication purposes under certain circumstances, even in the English-speaking world.

Language Activity Sheet

Writing Letters: Formal and Informal

Informal Letter Matrix: Make Three Lists

People I Know	Questions I Can Ask	This is What I Can Tell People

Formal Letter Matrix: Make Three Lists

Sources of Information	Who to Contact	Things I Would Like to Know

Appendix

Organizing for Long-Term Instruction

Teaching writing is about ensuring that students become better writers by learning something every day about writing well, and then practicing what they learn. The only way to ensure that this happens is to teach attributes of good writing every day. There are attributes of good writing addressed throughout the **Get Writing!!** series. They include:

- Thinking and writing in sentences and understanding the relationships between and among main ideas in sentences
- Thinking and writing in larger main ideas and understanding the relationships between and among main sentences
- Understanding the role of main ideas in paragraphs
- Thinking and writing in a variety of genres
- Progressively mastering the discipline of conventional writing

Organizing for long-term instruction is based on these factors:

1. **Mission Statement** (see below): Create a mission statement for the year. The mission statement must be about the students' writing performance and should be shared with the students. The mission statement articulates what students will be able to do by the end of the year and how that will be measured and reported. The mission statement must involve everyone in the room and include all students, individually and collectively. It is not limited to the average child in the room.
2. **Assessment** (p. 127-132): The teacher needs a way or ways to assess and measure writing behaviors that address the mission statement.
3. **Reporting** (p. 131): The teacher needs a way to report individual achievement of the mission statement to individual students, parents, administrators, and members of the district's governing board.
4. **Planning** (p. 133-136): To ensure achievement of the mission, the teacher must know what both the teacher and the students will do each month, week, and day.

Sample Mission Statement

The children will be able to develop ideas and use procedures appropriate for writing short fiction, reports of information, opinion essays, and autobiographical incidents or vignettes. They will write in sufficient quantity* every school day to include the genres above, as well as responses to their reading, daily journal reflections, and writing across the curriculum. The quality of student writing will increase as measured by sentence maturity, control over the conventions of standard English writing, as well as clarity and organization.

*To ensure sufficient quantity, establish a daily general word-count criterion. For example, it is reasonable to expect fifth-grade students to write as much as 850-1000 running words per day, or eight to ten pages. Set the baseline expectation at six pages of accumulated writing for the first two months of the year, and increase it to ten pages by the end of the year. Most of that writing is practice. It must be monitored, but it does not have to be read, scored, graded, noted with marginal messages, or sent home to be signed.

The emphasis here is on the teacher. The teacher must forge a *systematic* writing instruction program in his/her classroom. Without a systematic instructional program the children's writing won't be appreciably better at the end of the year than it was at the beginning.

Appendix

Assessment

Assessment in the Balanced Writing Program

Assessment is an integral part of all fundamental teaching. In reading assessment, we all essentially agree to look for word attack and comprehension. In mathematics assessment, we all essentially agree that we should observe numeration, operations, measurement, probability, statistics, and problem solving. But in writing, you may not agree with our ideas for assessment and we may not agree with yours. Likewise, the National Council of Teachers of English may not agree with the ideas of the *New York Times* or the Midwest Committee on Workplace Literacy, if there is such a group.

There is a serious implication here: *If no one agrees, there is no formal, relatively uniform assessment frame of reference, no relatively uniform assessment schedule or process.* The result? We all teach to whatever we determine should be the tests of writing quality, which can mean anything anyone decides it should mean. And if quality can mean anything, in practical application, it means nothing.

What is Quality Writing?

List what you look for and how you assess student writing. There are only seven spaces below. That doesn't mean there are only seven items. If you need more space, continue writing on a separate sheet.

1.

2.

3.

4.

5.

6.

7.

Appendix

Assessment

 The Scoring System

The following list includes three items which we (your authors) look for in student writing samples. Understand however, that these are not the only measure of writing ability.

1. **Fluency,** or ***How much did the child write?*** Fluency can be measured by counting the words the student wrote in a specified amount of time (**x** words in **y** minutes). Fluency is not a measure of writing quality, but it's important to recognize that without fluency, a writer's chance of producing quality writing is severely compromised.
2. **Maturity,** or ***What is the syntactic sophistication of the sentences the child wrote?*** Maturity can be measured by dividing the number of words the child wrote by the number of sentences. We can measure maturity by counting the clauses in the writing sample and dividing the number of clauses by the number of sentences. Complexity is not, by itself, a measure of quality in writing. But as young writers develop, their ideas get more sophisticated, and they need more sophisticated and complex ways to structure their ideas in writing.
3. **Mechanical Control,** or ***To what extent does the writing sample display the structure and discipline that makes written language work?*** Mechanical control can be measured by counting errors in capitalization, punctuation, spelling, usage, and sentence construction. We can then total the errors and divide the total by the number of sentences.

 Questions and Answers

Look over the items on your list (p. 127) and on our list. Then ask yourself the following questions:

1. *Does each item lead directly and predictably to the ability to write well?*
2. *To what extent can you measure—not evaluate or judge, but quantify—the items on your lists so you can assess them again and chart progress after several weeks of instruction?*

Here are our answers to these two questions:

1. No one learns to write well without writing something. Our three assessment items lead directly and predictably to writing well because they cause the child to write something. The quality of writing is carried, to a large extent, in sentence maturity appropriate to audience and purpose. As children mature, their audiences tend to mature, and their purposes tend to get more sophisticated.
2. Communication in writing depends on readers; and readers can understand what is being communicated, to a large extent, because writers make print follow certain capitalization, punctuation, spelling, usage, and sentence patterns. Thus, writing is called "good," to some extent, because it is mechanically accurate.

Each of our assessment items can be counted, thus quantified and measured again. A second assessment will show what the children learned on the three measures of writing ability.

As the writers of this book, we cannot specify what your assessment variables should be. We can, however, recommend different ways to look at assessment, such as the following, based on the analytic criteria: **fluency**, **maturity**, and **mechanical control**.

 The First Monday Assessment

On the first Monday of the year, collect a writing sample for analytic assessment. Direct students to write a journal entry about something they learned recently, something they did that made them feel good, something they taught someone else to do, something they know how to do. Focus on this type of topic—children are experts on themselves.

Students will often ask if spelling counts. Tell them that spelling always counts: "Spell as well as you can all the time, but don't stop writing just because you don't know how to spell a word. If you come to a word you think you don't know how to spell, use enough of the right letters so you'll be able to read it later, and then make it right."

If students ask about punctuation, tell them it always counts and to always write as well as they can. Tell them also that if they come to a place where they are not sure what to do, to try their best, then make a mark at the end of the line and go back to it later and make it right. But to never stop writing just because they don't know what punctuation mark to use.

 The Writing Sample

Prepare students for assessment by making sure they have paper and pencil or pen. If your students use word processors, set them up, individually, at a keyboard and screen. Tell them that you will give them the topic, and they will write "as much as they can as well as they can." Then prompt a writing sample, getting them to think by giving oral suggestions. **Note**: This is all oral on the teacher's part and mental on the children's.

Example: Mentally take them into their home. On this imaginary tour, they walk around the house and feel what it's like to be there. They look into all the rooms. They choose one room, any room, and go inside. They look around. Direct them to think about why they chose that room.

Ask them to think about what's in the room, who tends to be there, what is done there. Ask them to think about all the things they know about that room. Say, "Boys and girls, I want you to write about that room in your house. You may write in whatever way you wish, but you are to write as much as you can as well as you can. You have five minutes. [Pause a count or two.] Begin."

Nearly every child will begin to write at this prompt. The few who raise their hand for clarification can be answered simply with the direction, "Do you have a room? Choose a room in your house. Write about that room." If the child tells you that (s)he can't think of anything, simply encourage.

If a child writes nothing, that's the score for this initial assessment. This isn't unfair. If you're assessing reading and the child doesn't read, there is nothing to assess, so you wait for the next time. No effort, no behavior, or no production, is an assessment. Don't be concerned. It's the rare child who writes nothing, and we've never seen it happen twice.

Appendix

Assessment

 The First Week Assessment

During the first week of school, collect one more writing sample. Give students only five minutes to write this sample. Make sure every student has the same amount of time to write. (**Note:** See p. 128-129 for directions in taking and scoring a writing sample.) Prompt a writing sample as below.

Example: Write a two-word character description on the board (***old man***, for instance). Direct the children to think of a sentence that contains the idea of old man, but tell them they need not use those words to express the idea. Listen to several sentences, then write ***weather*** on the board and direct them to think of a sentence that contains both the ideas, ***old man*** and ***weather*** (they need not use those words). Listen to several again, then direct students to write on paper the sentence they have written in their heads. Remind them that writers always write as well as they can. Allow about one minute for the writing, then solicit readings.

Write the word ***vehicle*** on the board. Have students include the idea of vehicle into their sentence somewhere. Listen to several sentences. Now, put the numeral **1** beside ***weather*** on the board. Put a **2** beside ***vehicle*** and a **3** beside ***old man***, and instruct students to write a new sentence in which the three ideas appear in that order. Their new sentence will be their ticket to recess. During the recess break, read their sentences, paying special attention to sentences that work particularly well and are mechanically accurate.

Post the sentences that work best on the Best Effort Board so students can see this work when they get back from recess. Direct their attention to the Best Effort Board, and tell them that they are responsible for deciding what their best effort is each day so they can post their own work. Explain that they will write every day so everyone will have best efforts every day.

 Follow-Up Assessment

To determine whether the objectives related to fluency and mechanical control have been satisfied or at least approached, the teacher might conduct a five-minute writing sample on Friday of the second week.

 Scoring the Sample and Reporting

When the children finish their writing sample, direct them to count the words they wrote and put the number in a circle at the top of their paper. Then collect the papers. Using the three-part scoring system (p. 128), determine the scores for each writing sample and record the results on the assessment form, one set of scores per sheet. The reason for two samples is that children have good days and not-so-good days. They also write better to some cues or situations than others. By writing two times under two circumstances, the average of the week's samples is a better gauge of how the children write than a single sample.

Important Note: A total of two to three hours of analytic assessment in a whole year, to identify baseline performance, establish instructional objectives, and show the magnitude of progress, is a reasonable amount of time. This data can also show the parents, the principal, the board of education, and the local newspaper that the children are learning to write well.

Before you throw your hands up and say there isn't time in your day to do this, remember that the time consumed in most assessment processes is vastly front-loaded. That is, if it takes an hour to do running records on 10 children, the first four children consume 30 minutes, and the other six are done in the last thirty minutes. We all know that we get better with practice. With practice, this analytic writing sample assessment system takes between thirty and fifty seconds to complete for each child.

The practice is usually about six samples. Therefore, after scoring about six children, you'll be doing each one in under one minute. That's about thirty to forty minutes for the class. Two samples in the first week demands about 70-90 minutes. Another analytic assessment will not be necessary until about midyear, and then again at the end of the year, and then with one sample each time.

 First Week Analytic Assessment: A Class Scenario

These are very plausible average figures for a first week of analytic assessment:

# Words:	**35**
# Sentences:	**5**
# Clauses:	**6**
Word/Snt:	**7.0 (35 words divided by 5 sentences)**
Clauses/Snt:	**1.2 (6 clauses divided by 5 sentences)**
Total Errors:	**9**
Errors/Snt:	**1.8 (9 mechanical errors divided by 5 sentences)**

In five minutes, this class of fourth graders writes an average of 35 words in an average of 5 essentially simple sentences. The average number of words per sentence is 7; the average number of clauses per sentence is 1.2, or about one multiple-clause sentence in every five. On the average, there are 9 errors per sample, or 1.8 per average sentence. Of course, there are children in the room who write up to 50-60 words, some who write an error-free draft, some who write compound, even complex sentences. Other fourth-graders write only three to five words and commit many errors. But the averages are those that appear above.

Based on these averages, the teacher establishes two objectives for the following two months:

1. Increase number of words per sentence to 40 or more
2. Decrease error rate to 1.5 or less

Writing Assessment Worksheet

Date: ____________________

Student Names	#Words	#Sentences	#Clauses	#Words/ Sentences	Clauses/ Sentences	Cp	Pn	Sp	SNT Errors*	E/S
Averages**										

*Cp: Capitalization errors
Pn: Punctuation Errors
Sp: Spelling Errors
SNT: Sentence Structure Errors (Fragments, Run-ons, and Usage)
E/S: Total Errors divided by Number of Sentences Equals Errors per Sentence (E/S)

** Totals divided by number of writing samples provides a baseline for establishing a two- or three-month objective. (For example, if the the average number of words is 32, the objective may be to increase the class average by 10% in two months, 10% more in next two months, and 10% more by the end of the year.

Appendix

Sample Instruction Plans

One-Year Writing Instruction Plan

The sample one-year instructional plan on p. 135 begins with specification of genre study by the month. It is important to note that when a specific genre is identified for a month (e.g., September - Biography Report of Information), it means that the report of information is a focus, and students are writing those reports, whether one major report in the month, or several shorter ones. We recommend several shorter ones, perhaps as many as two individually and two in dyads or triads, each report limited to as few as two handwritten pages, or 150-200 words.

Note to Teacher: Please keep in mind that this plan is a prototype. If a genre is not represented (e.g., poetry, journals), and must be, make the proper adjustments.

One-Month Writing Instruction Plan

A sample one-month instruction plan for October appears on p. 136. This is a sample, or prototype breakout from the sample one-year plan.

Note to Teacher: If a genre is not represented in this plan (e.g., poetry, journals), and a teacher feels it must be, adjustments can be made.

Please note the following elements in this plan:

- Everyone in the class has a short fiction piece in progress at all times throughout the year. There is never a time when students are not beginning a story, working on a story, finishing a story, reading a story aloud (in Writers' Workshop, for example), revising a story, or publishing a story. All research writing is cooperative and can occur in any curricular area.
- Students are engaged in a variety of genres at once.
- Students are working on the discipline of constructing the language and mastering age-appropriate mechanical control.
- The breakout appears as four five-day weeks, from day to day throughout the month.

At first, this plan may appear rather lock-step. Using this approach, however, an enormous amount and variety of direct instruction and practice in the art and craft of writing can be accomplished in a school year. In this sample month, students write four biographical reports of information, four formal letters, at least one story, one research report, and numerous formal sentences and paragraphs.

This a lot of writing for students at this level, but it is well within their concentration and production capacity. If they aren't interested, there is always a risk that they will find the quantity unreasonable. However, in this program, students tailor the genre writing to their preferences: they select their biographical focus, the audience for their letters, and the questions for their research.

The biggest motivational problem in any skill or subject area in school is competence—students who do well are motivated and students who don't aren't motivated. However, with sufficient work, as outlined in this sample month, the probability that every child will write progressively well increases.

Appendix

One-Month Instruction Plan

 Reading Biographies

Each week in the sample plan begins with biography reading in preparation for writing the weekly report of information (Objective 10, Book 2). If this plan is followed, students will write approximately 35 reports of information on biographical figures during the year. Because they share these reports every Friday and learn about different people, they will know several dozen influential figures well by the end of the year. Biographical reading can be drawn from history, politics, multicultural education, the arts, literature, and so forth. The weekly reports of information also greatly enhance content-area learning.

On Monday, focus on Power Writing (Objective 22 in ***Get Writing!! Book 2 Grades 4-5***). To that end, conduct Power Writing on Monday, Wednesday, and Thursday of the week and use the revision portion of Power Writing on both Wednesday and Thursday. In addition, focus on sentence writing (Objective 1 and 2, Book 1) and paragraph awareness and writing (Objective 2, Book 2).

Throughout sentence and paragraph awareness and writing, call attention to the relationship between mechanical accuracy and meaning-making in sentences (Objectives 7, 9, 10, 11, and 12, as needed). Also, between Tuesday and Friday, everyone in the class will write at least two informal letters (Objective 14, Book 2).

 Fiction Writing at Least Twice a Week

In this plan, everyone is working on short fiction at least two times during the week. Everyone will write one formal (business) letter (Objective 16, Book 2), and the spelling program will be enhanced by Objectives 8 and/or 15.

 Fridays

In each of the four Fridays in the sample plan, there are two major activities: the sharing of biographical reports and a formal review of capitalization and punctuation. We encourage teachers to make sharing a biographical report of information a major event. In an event such as "The Biography Faire," students might enhance their presentations of dates and achievements in a dramatic performance (e.g., choral reading, dramatic performance, or reading a portion of a great speech). The point is to give the biographical figures some life, something that they will remember.

We certainly do not intend for mechanical control to be relegated to the end of the week, in isolation from the rest of the writing week. On the contrary, Friday is intended as a time when capitalization and punctuation conventions can be addressed formally, so that afterward such mechanical devices can be referred to and practiced in the context of the larger process of writing. (Read Objectives 11 and 12 for a detailed explanation of content.)

We encourage teachers to make downward adjustments in production expectations only when it is apparent that the children cannot keep up, and then only with those students who cannot keep up.

Sample One-Year Writing Calendar

Month	Genres	Construction	Mechanical Control
September	Biography Report of Information Autobiographical Incident (Weekly)	Single Sentence #1-#2-#3, Double Sentence #4 Triple Sentence #4-#5, Multiple Sentences #1 (Bk 2)	General Review #10 Spelling #8 and #15
October	Biography Report of Information Cooperative Research Formal Letter (Weekly) Fiction On-Going	Complex Sentence #6, Sentence Combining #9 Paragraphing #2	Capitalization and Punctuation #11-#12 Spelling #8 and #15
November	Biography Report Autobiographical Incident (Weekly) Fiction On-Going	Compound Sentences #7, Sentence Combining #9 Paragraphing #2-#3	Capitalization and Punctuation #11-#12 Spelling #8 and #15
December	Biography Report of Information Cooperative Research	Compound/Complex Sentences #6-7 Paragraphing #3-#4-#5	Capitalization and Punctuation #11-#12 Spelling #8 and #15
January	Biography Report of Information Autobiographical Incident (Weekly) Opinion Essay Fiction On-Going	Sentences with Modifiers #14, Paragraphing #3 Paragraph-a-Day #6	Review Capitalization and Punctuation #10-#11-#12 Spelling #8 and #15
February	Biography Report of Information Cooperative Research Formal Letter (Weekly) Fiction On-Going	Sentences with Modifiers #14 Sentences with Pronouns #13 Paragraphing #3 Paragraph-a-Day #6	Review Capitalization and Punctuation #10-#11-#12 Spelling #8 and #15
March	Biography Report of Information Autobiographical Incident (Weekly) Persuasive Essay Fiction On-Going	Sentences with Modifiers #14 Sentences with Pronouns #13 Paragraphing #3 Paragraph-a-Day #6	Capitalization and Punctuation as Needed Spelling #8 and #15
April	Biography Report of Information Cooperative Research Informal Letter (Weekly) Fiction On-Going	Sentences with Pronouns #13 Review Sentencing #1-#2-#3-#4-#5-#6-#7 Paragraph-a-Day #6	Responsibility for Capitalization and- Punctuation #10-#11-#12 Spelling #8 and ##15
May	Biography Report of Information Autobiographical Incident (Weekly) Persuasive Essay Fiction Closure	Paragraph-a-Day #6	Editing Portfolio for Mechanical Control Spelling #8 and #15
June	Final Organization and preparation of portfolio for Literacy Faire		Application of all conventions to final revision of materials for Literacy Faire

Sample One-Month Calendar

	Monday	Tuesday	Wednesday	Thursday	Friday
Week One	• Read Biographies • Fiction Writing at least twice in the week #18 • Spelling #8 and #15 during the week	• Read Biographies • Complex Sentences #16	• Plan Biographical Report of Information #10 • Paragraphing #2	• Write Report of Information • Complex Sentences in Reports #16	• Complete and Share Reports of Information #10 • Capitalization/Punctuation #11-#12
Week Two	• Read Biographies • Fiction Writing at least twice in the week #7-#8 • One Formal Letter this week #16 • Spelling #8 and #15 during the week	• Read Biographies • Set Up Cooperative Research #9 • Complex Sentences embedded in genres • Paragraphing #2	• Plan Biographical Report of Information #10 • Conduct Research • Sentence Combining #9 • Paragraphing #2	• Write Report of Information #10 • Conduct Research • Sentence Combining #9	• Complete and Share Reports of Information #10 • Capitalization/Punctuation #11-#12
Week Three	• Read Biographies • Fiction Writing at least twice in the week #7-#8 • One Formal Letter this week #16 • Spelling #8 and #15 during the week	• Read Biographies • Writing Research Report #9 • Sentence Combining and Complex Sentences embedded in Genres	• Plan Biographical Report of Information #10 • Writing Research Report #9 • Sentence Combining and Complex Sentences embedded in Genres	• Write Report of Information • Writing Research Report #9	• Complete and Share Reports of Information #11-#12 • Capitalization/Punctuation #11-#12
Week Four	• Read Biographies • Fiction Writing at least twice in the week #7-#8 • One Formal Letter this week #16 • Spelling #8 and #15 during the week	• Read Biographies • Research Report • Class Sharing • Sentence Combining and Complex Sentences embedded in Genres	• Plan Biographical Report of Information #10 • Research Report • Class Sharing	• Write Report of Information	• Complete and Share Reports of Information #10 • Capitalization/Punctuation #11-#12

Bibliography

Farnan, N., D. Rocha-Hill, and L. Fearn. (1994). *We Can All Write*. San Diego: Kabyn Books.

Farnan, N., E. Goldman, and L. Fearn. (1985). *Developing Writers in Grades 7 - 12*. San Diego: Kabyn Books.

Farnan, N. and L. Fearn. (1994). "The Writing Program in Action: A Writer's Ruminations about Portfolios," *Writing Teacher*, VII, May, 26-27.

Fearn, L. (1976). "Individual Development: A Process Model in Creativity," *Journal of Creative Behavior*, 10 , 55-64.

_______. (1981). *(The First) First I Think*. San Diego: Kabyn Books.

_______. (1981). "Teaching Writing by Teaching Thinking." *Academic Therapy*, 17:173-178

Fearn, L. and K. Foster. (1979). *The Writing Kabyn*. San Diego: Kabyn Books.

Prior, J. A. (1979). "The Impact of Developmental Writing Instruction on Learning Handicapped Students." Unpublished Masters Degree Thesis, San Diego: San Diego State University.

Notes

Notes

Notes

Notes

Notes

Reading, Writing, Thinking Gr. Pre-K–9

★ Structures for Reading, Writing, Thinking

Gr. 4-9

Finally, a complete teaching program for improving students' reading, writing, and thinking skills. Each book in this series stands alone, but together they provide a comprehensive curriculum for reading, writing, and thinking in the content areas.

Book 1-Expository text structures and three types of paragraphs: sequential, enumerative, and descriptive. **Book 2**-Expository text structures and three types of paragraphs: compare/contrast, cause/effect, and problem/solution. **Book 3**-Research and report writing. **Book 4**-Content-area reading and writing.

ECS0549	Book 1	160 pp.	$17.95
ECS0557	Book 2	160 pp.	$17.95
ECS0565	Book 3	144 pp.	$16.95
ECS0573	Book 4	112 pp.	$14.95

★ Writing Warm-Ups™
Writing Warm-Ups™ Two

Gr. K-6

Writing Warm-Ups™ are brief and creative writing activities for teachers who want students to make the most of every minute in the classroom. Warm-ups are quick, convenient writing exercises that encourage students to enjoy and play with words. **80 pp. each**

ECS9072	Writing Warm-Ups™	$10.95
ECS9455	Writing Warm-Ups™ Two	$10.95

★ **Best Sellers**

Passageways
Creative Lessons to Improve Writing & Vocabulary Skills

Gr. 5-9

Passageways offers an enjoyable alternative to the dull, repetitive vocabulary exercises found in many textbooks. The activities challenge students to develop an enthusiasm for words while gaining a deeper understanding of language and enhancing the overall quality of written expression. Three vocabulary lists are provided for a range of reading levels. However, activities are designed so they can be used with almost any general vocabulary list. **96 pp.**

ECS9625	Passageways	$12.95

The Picture Book Companion
Books I, II, and III,

Gr. K-3

Imagine being able to create a community of readers in your classroom. *The Picture Book Companion* series is designed to do just that. Each book in this series provides reading teachers with 45 classroom-tested study guides for the best of children's picture books. Each lesson includes prereading questions, vocabulary words, postreading questions, and activities for brainstorming, creative writing, and art. **96 pp. each**

ECS9587	The Picture Book Companion, I	$12.95
ECS9595	The Picture Book Companion, II	$12.95
ECS9641	The Picture Book Companion, III	$12.95

★ Springboards for Reading

Gr. 3-6

These lessons serve as springboards for developing students' strategic reading skills. Each lesson addresses a particular reading skill in a "non-textbook" manner and emphasizes active student involvement through reading, discussion, cooperative learning, creative and critical thinking, and other motivating activities. The lessons focus on six important areas of understanding and skill: Vocabulary, facts and details, main idea, causal relationships, inferences, and fact/nonfact. **96 pp.**

ECS9692	Springboards for Reading	$11.95

Novel Extenders

Books 1, 2, 3, 4, Gr. 1-3
African-American Collection, Gr. 4-6
Multicultural Collection, Gr. 1-3, Gr. 4-6

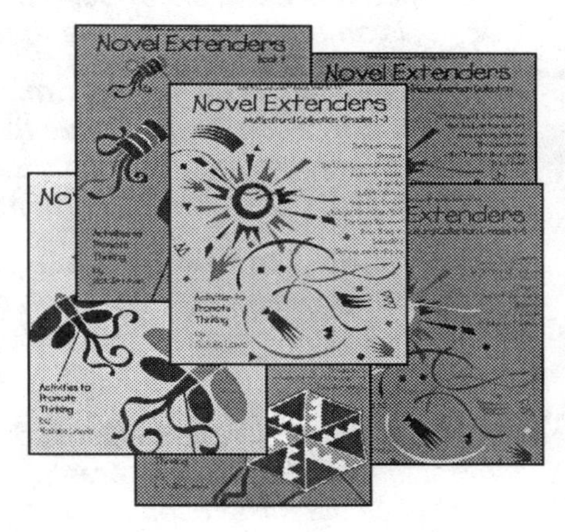

Take your children beyond the common vocabulary and simple comprehension tests when teaching popular children's literature. *Novel Extenders* include activities that will help children further explore various aspects of literature (setting, plot, story ending) in many creative, challenging ways. Each *Novel Extenders* contains activities for various children's books. Included is a cover page with book summary, recommended grade level, and suggestions to connect the book to other topics, ideas, or concepts in the curriculum. Literature selections are easy to find. **112 - 144 pp.**

ECS000X	Novel Extenders, Book 1	$15.95
ECS0018	Novel Extenders, Book 2	$16.95
ECS0069	Novel Extenders, Book 3	$15.95
ECS0077	Novel Extenders, Book 4	$15.95
ECS0506	Novel Extenders: African-American Collection,Gr. 4-6	$14.95
ECS0603	Novel Extenders: Multicultural Collection,Gr. 1-3	$14.95
ECS0786	Novel Extenders: Multicultural Collection	$14.95

To order, contact your local school supply store, or write:

ECS Learning Systems, Inc.
P.O. Box 791437
San Antonio, TX 78279-1437